GCSE

Oxford Literature Companions

Romeo and Juliet

WILLIAM SHAKESPEARE

WORKBOOK

Notes and activities: Adrian Cropper
Series consultant: Peter Buckroyd

OXFORD
UNIVERSITY PRESS

Contents

Introduction

What are Oxford Literature Companions?

Oxford Literature Companions is a series designed to provide you with comprehensive support for popular set texts. You can use the Companion workbook alongside your play, using relevant sections during your studies or using the workbook as a whole for revision. The workbook will help you to create your own personalized guide to the text.

What are the main features within this workbook?

Each workbook in the Oxford Literature Companion series follows the same approach and includes the following features:

Activities

Each workbook offers a range of varied and in-depth activities to deepen understanding and encourage close work with the text, covering characters, themes, language, performance and context. The Skills and Practice chapter also offers advice on assessment and includes sample questions and student answers. There are spaces to write your answers throughout the workbook.

Key terms and quotations

Throughout the workbook, key terms are highlighted in the text and explained on the same page. There is also a detailed glossary at the end of the workbook that explains, in the context of the play, all the relevant literary terms highlighted.

Quotations from the play appear in blue text throughout this workbook.

Upgrade

As well as providing guidance on key areas of the play, throughout this workbook you will also find 'Upgrade' features. These are tips to help with your exam preparation and performance.

Progress check

Each chapter of the workbook ends with a 'Progress check'. Through self-assessment, these enable you to establish how confident you feel about what you have been learning and help you to set next steps and targets.

Which edition of the play has this workbook used?

Quotations have been taken from the Oxford University Press edition of *Romeo and Juliet* (ISBN 978-0-19-832166-8).

Plot and Structure

Plot

Romeo and Juliet is a play that explores the highly charged subject of love. Set in medieval Verona, the plot focuses on the relationship between the 'star-cross'd lovers' *(Prologue)*, Romeo (a Montague) and Juliet (a Capulet). The **tragedy** of the play is not only the deaths of the young **protagonists**, but the fact that the lesson of tolerance is only learned by the families through the pain and grief caused by their loss.

The Prologue

The **Prologue**, written in **sonnet** form, directly addresses the audience and prepares them for the action and content of the play. The **Chorus** acts as a commentator for the action to follow and a guide to how the writer may expect the audience to feel about what they experience.

> **Chorus** in Elizabethan drama, an actor who recites the Prologue and may comment at other times on the action of the play
>
> **Prologue** in drama, an introductory scene, often written in verse, that establishes the themes, plot or characters of the play; from the Greek *pro* (before) and *logos* (word)
>
> **protagonist(s)** the main character(s)
>
> **sonnet** a 14-line poem with a formal rhyme scheme and condensed form; often for expressing strong emotions, particularly love; in Shakespearean sonnets the rhyme scheme is ABABCDCDEFEFGG
>
> **tragedy** a drama dealing with serious themes, ending in the suffering or death of one or more of the principal characters

Activity 1

Read the following descriptions of some of the things we learn from the Prologue and find suitable short quotations to match them:

Both families are of similar importance   --

Their argument is rooted in the past   --

People outside the family are hurt   --

Romeo and Juliet are born   --

The unlucky tragic accidents they face   --

The argument is ended   --

The events on stage   --

The efforts of the actors   --

Activity 2

Why do you think that Shakespeare felt the need for the use of the Prologue in
Romeo and Juliet? Why not just start the play with the dramatic first scene?
Write a paragraph to explain your thoughts.

Act 1, Scene 1

The main focus of the scene is to present the two warring families in Verona: the
Capulets and the Montagues. Shakespeare does this by showing the effect of the
feud (the conflict) from the **perspective** of characters outside the two families.
We are also introduced to Romeo.

perspective a
particular opinion or
point of view that is
dependent on personal
interests or beliefs

> **Key quotations**
>
> 'What, drawn and talk of peace? I hate the word,
> As I hate hell, all Montagues, and thee.' *(Tybalt)*

Activity 3

What does the audience learn about Romeo from the way he explains his feelings
to Benvolio? Complete the table below to gather your ideas. You could also look for
other evidence in this part of the scene.

Evidence	What this says about Romeo
'Griefs of mine own lie heavy in my breast'	
'Love is a smoke made with the fume of sighs'	
'Tut, I have lost myself, I am not here, This is not Romeo, he's some other where'	
'she'll not be hit / With Cupid's arrow'	
'She will not stay the siege of loving terms'	
'She is too fair, too wise, wisely too fair, To merit bliss by making me despair'	
'O teach me how I should forget to think'	

Activity 4

Now write a description of Romeo based on how he is discussed by his mother, father and friend, but also how he presents himself when talking to Benvolio.

Using quotations to support your ideas

You should always use some textual evidence to support your ideas. Make sure that the quotations are brief and are integrated into your own ideas. For example:

Benvolio is determined to help his friend and asks him to 'Examine other beauties' so that he will think about someone else other than Rosaline.

Act 1, Scene 2

Lord Capulet asks Paris to wait two years before he marries Juliet or to prove that she loves him and gives him consent at the party being held that night. Romeo is persuaded by Benvolio to attend the party – uninvited.

> **Key quotations**
>
> 'She hath not seen the change of fourteen years;' *(Lord Capulet)*
>
> 'Take thou some new infection to thy eye,
> And the rank poison of the old will die.' *(Benvolio)*

Activity 5

Find evidence from this scene for the following:

- how Paris persuades Lord Capulet
- how Benvolio persuades Romeo.

You should choose extracts that demonstrate persuasive language and then explain how the text is persuasive; an example has been done for you below:

Evidence	How this language is persuasive
'Of honourable reckoning are you both, And pity 'tis, you liv'd at odds so long.'	Paris' language persuades Lord Capulet that he is a respectful young man when he speaks about Lord Capulet and Lord Montague using the word 'honourable'.

Act 1, Scene 3

Lady Capulet introduces Juliet to the subject of Paris as a suitable husband in terms of family, wealth and attractiveness. The Nurse, who has been a second mother to Juliet, is also very enthusiastic about the prospects of this **dynastic marriage**.

Juliet shows that she is a dutiful and loyal daughter in agreeing to her mother's request.

dynastic marriage
a marriage that strengthens family links; here, the Capulets will be linked to the family of Prince Escales if Paris and Juliet marry

Key quotations

'Well, think of marriage now; younger than you, Here in Verona, ladies of esteem, Are made already mothers.' *(Lady Capulet)*

'What say you, can you love the gentleman?' *(Lady Capulet)*

Activity 6

We have briefly been introduced to Lady Capulet in the first scene when she tries to stop her husband involving himself in the street-fight. In Scene 3, we learn a lot more about her character as well as being introduced to the Nurse and Juliet.

Write a description of Lady Capulet, the Nurse and Juliet and what we learn about them, based on the way they are presented in this scene.

You may wish to use some of the following words to support your thoughts:

affectionate   willing   proud   loyal   businesslike

understanding   distant   close   caring   emotional

loving   maternal   empathy   persuasive   enthusiastic

Lady Capulet -

- -

- -

- -

Nurse -

- -

- -

Juliet -

- -

- -

Act 1, Scene 4

Benvolio and Mercutio struggle to persuade Romeo to attend the Capulet party. Mercutio goes to great lengths to explore the significance of dreams in order to defeat Romeo's reluctance and ensure that he accompanies them.

> **Key quotations**
>
> 'Is love a tender thing? it is too rough,
> Too rude, too boist'rous, and it pricks like thorn.' *(Romeo)*

Activity 7

Complete the spider diagram to identify the reasons Romeo gives in this scene for not wishing to go to the Capulet party.

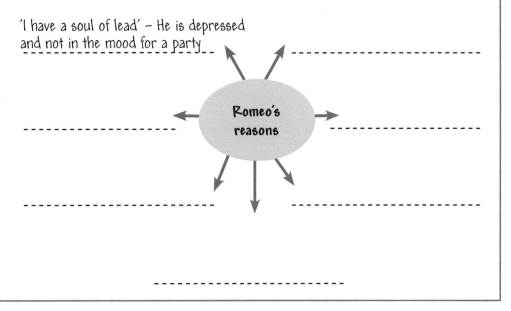

'I have a soul of lead' – He is depressed and not in the mood for a party

Romeo's reasons

Act 1, Scene 5

Tybalt sees Romeo at the party and wants to challenge him but is prevented by Lord Capulet, who says that Romeo is a respected man in Verona. Romeo forgets Rosaline as he and Juliet meet and fall instantly in love. They separately discover that the other is part of an enemy family.

Key quotations

'I will withdraw, but this intrusion shall,
Now seeming sweet, convert to bitt'rest gall.' *(Tybalt)*

'My lips, two blushing pilgrims, ready stand
To smooth that rough touch with a tender kiss.' *(Romeo)*

'Then have my lips the sin that they have took.' *(Juliet)*

Activity 8

Answer the following questions, which consider the character of Tybalt and the role of the Montague–Capulet feud.

a) Explain how you think the character Tybalt will be feeling after he leaves the scene and what this may lead to.

b) Why do you think that Shakespeare presented Romeo and Juliet's realisation of each other's family background at the *end* of the scene?

----

c) What is interesting about what Lord Capulet says about Romeo to Tybalt in the first part of the scene?

Activity 9

The speech given by the Chorus in sonnet form that appears at the end of Act 1 offers an overview of the situation at this point of the play. It focuses on the changes and the problems the lovers now face.

a) Work through the speech set out here and highlight each change or difficulty. Explain the changes or difficulties that Romeo and Juliet face. The first one has been done to get you started.

Chorus

Now old desire doth in his death-bed lie,

And young affection gapes to be his heir;

That fair for which love groan'd for and would die,

With tender Juliet match'd is now not fair.

Now Romeo is belov'd, and loves again,

Alike bewitched by the charm of looks;

But to his foe suppos'd he must complain,

And she steal love's sweet bait from fearful hooks.

Being held a foe, he may not have access

To breathe such vows as lovers use to swear,

And she as much in love, her means much less

To meet her new belov'd any where:

But passion lends them power, time means, to meet,

Temp'ring extremities with extreme sweet.

Refers to Rosaline, his first love.

b) Now sum up the speech in one sentence.

Act 2, Scene 1

Romeo returns to Juliet. Mercutio presents a very different view of love in his comic speech. He focuses on the humour of the way love can change a person and refers to Rosaline, Romeo's earlier love. He and Benvolio are unaware that Romeo has fallen in love with Juliet.

> **Key quotations**
>
> 'Can I go forward when my heart is here?' *(Romeo)*
>
> 'If love be blind, love cannot hit the mark.' *(Mercutio)*

Act 2, Scene 2

Shakespeare allows both Juliet and Romeo openly to declare their feelings to themselves in this scene through the use of **soliloquy**.

soliloquy where a character voices aloud their innermost thoughts for the audience to hear

> **Key quotations**
>
> 'It is my lady, O it is my love:
> O that she knew she were!' *(Romeo)*
>
> 'What's in a name? That which we call a rose
> By any other name would smell as sweet;' *(Juliet)*

Activity 10

In this important scene there are some presentational features that help the audience to empathise more closely with the characters. Explore your thoughts in the following two questions:

a) Why is it important that the audience is able to hear the independent thoughts of Romeo and Juliet? Why is it important that Romeo hears Juliet's thoughts before he speaks to her?

----

b) What rules of courtship have been broken by what has happened in this scene? How is this expressed by Juliet in particular? (Clue – look at her speeches beginning with the lines: 'Thou knowest the mask of night', 'Or if thou thinkst I am too quickly won' and 'I should have been more strange'.)

----

c) Now look at the quotations below – who is expressing their love, Romeo or Juliet? Write 'R' or 'J' in the boxes. Try to complete this without looking back at the play!

'look thou but sweet,' [------]

'call me but love,' [------]

'If thou dost love, pronounce it faithfully;' [------]

'swear by thy gracious self,' [------]

'all this is but a dream,' [------]

'My bounty is as boundless as the sea, / My love as deep;' [------]

'Parting is such sweet sorrow,' [------]

'Th'exchange of thy love's faithful vow for mine.' [------]

'Yet I should kill thee with much cherishing.' [------]

'I will not fail, 'tis twenty year till then.' [------]

'O that I were a glove upon that hand,' [------]

'And but thou love me,' [------]

Act 2, Scene 3

Eager to organise his planned marriage to Juliet, Romeo visits his **confidant**, Friar Lawrence. The audience is introduced to his skills with herbal remedies before Romeo arrives. Friar Lawrence is well aware of the balance of positive and negative in nature and sees the impulsive marriage as a way of healing the wounds that prolong the feud between the Capulets and the Montagues.

> **confidant (m) / confidante (f)**
> someone who acts as a counsellor, someone to be trusted; the Nurse plays a similar role for Juliet for part of the play

Key quotations

' – thy earliness doth me assure
Thou art uprous'd with some distemp'rature;' *(Friar Lawrence)*

'Holy Saint Francis, what a change is here!' *(Friar Lawrence)*

Activity 11

In the dialogue between Romeo and his counsellor, Friar Lawrence, we learn a great deal about what has happened previously as well as about Romeo's present feelings. Find relevant references in the text to support each of the points in the table below.

Friar Lawrence's outlook	Relevant quotations
I know that you did not really love Rosaline.	
I think you are still obsessed with Rosaline.	
You wasted tears on Rosaline.	
Please don't nag me about it!	
How can you forget your first love so quickly?	

Act 2, Scene 4

Benvolio and Mercutio discuss the challenge to a duel (fight) delivered from Tybalt to Romeo. Mercutio's character and his humour dominate until the arrival of the Nurse. She has been sent as Juliet's representative to learn about the plans for the marriage.

> **Key quotations**
>
> 'Alas, poor Romeo, he is already dead, stabbed with a white wench's black eye,' *(Mercutio)*

Activity 12

In this scene, the Nurse is meeting Romeo properly for the first time. She has heard all about him from Juliet and is keen to make sure that he is suitable for her mistress. Match the following quotations with the corresponding description of her behaviour:

Description	Quotation
encouraging	'I am so vexed that every part about me quivers.'
shocked/insulted	'O, there is a nobleman in town, one Paris,'
suspicious/cautious	'And 'a speak any thing against me, I'll take him down,'
critical/nagging	'if you should deal double with her, truly it were an ill thing'
warning/challenging	'Is your man secret?'
gossiping	'Out upon you, what a man are you?'
angry	'And thou must stand by too and suffer every knave to use me...!'
defensive/assertive	'she looks as pale as any clout in the versal world.'

Activity 13

Now, with reference to your thoughts in response to Activity 6, explain how you think Shakespeare has developed the presentation of the Nurse in this scene. What *more* do we know about her?

Act 2, Scene 5

The Nurse takes her time to tease an impatient Juliet before finally giving her the good news about the marriage planned for later that day to be officiated by Friar Lawrence in secret.

Key quotations

'Then hie you hence to Friar Lawrence' cell,
There stays a husband to make you a wife.' *(Nurse)*

Activity 14

In this scene it is clear that the Nurse has been impressed by Romeo from the way she describes his physical features and character. Use the table below to note down how she praises him.

Physical features	Character qualities

Act 2, Scene 6

The scene moves to Friar Lawrence's cell, where the marriage is to take place. Romeo is eager to be married and Friar Lawrence is full of praise for the charms of Juliet.

 Activity 15

Romeo and Friar Lawrence have different priorities in this marriage scene.

a) Identify briefly what these priorities are.

i. Romeo: ---

----

ii. Friar Lawrence: ---

----

b) Find evidence for their different priorities and use this to help you write a detailed paragraph for each character explaining them. The paragraph for Romeo has been started for you.

i. Romeo: thinking for the moment

Romeo has his focus only on marrying Juliet and is not concerned with any negative consequences...

----

ii. Friar Lawrence: thinking for the future

Act 3, Scene 1

Romeo is confronted by Tybalt but refuses to fight him. Mercutio does not understand and sees this as dishonourable behaviour. He steps in to fight and is killed by Tybalt. Romeo is enraged: he confronts and kills Tybalt. As a punishment, Romeo is sent into exile from Verona by the Prince – he cannot return to the city without fear of imprisonment or death.

> **Key quotations**
>
> 'Romeo, the love I bear thee can afford
> No better term than this: thou art a villain.' *(Tybalt)*
>
> 'I do protest I never injuried thee,
> But love thee better than thou canst devise,' *(Romeo)*

Activity 16

This is a long scene. Put the following events in chronological order by placing a number in each box.

Romeo intervenes in the fight between Mercutio and Tybalt ` ------ `

Tybalt is killed ` ------ `

Mercutio dies ` ------ `

Romeo is consumed with rage ` ------ `

Lady Capulet believes that Benvolio is not a trustworthy witness as he is a Montague ` ------ `

Benvolio warns Mercutio that there are Capulets in the area ` ------ `

Mercutio is disrespectful to Tybalt ` ------ `

Romeo is exiled ` ------ `

Mercutio cannot accept Romeo's refusal to fight Tybalt ` ------ `

Romeo blames his love for Juliet for weakening him ` ------ `

Tybalt challenges Romeo ` ------ `

Lord Montague does not believe that his son deserves to die ` ------ `

Benvolio reminds everyone about the Prince's law against public fighting ` ------ `

Activity 17

a) Imagine that you are a prosecuting barrister in court. For each of the characters below, give your key reasons for accusing them of being the main cause of the death of Tybalt. One has been given in each case to start you off.

i. Romeo: reasons for guilt

He has killed a Capulet in a duel when the Prince banned fighting in the streets.

----

ii. Mercutio: reasons for guilt

He interrupted Tybalt and Romeo – it is possible that the fight may not have happened.

----

iii. Tybalt: reasons for guilt

He was determined to start the fight even after Lord Capulet told him to leave Romeo alone.

----

b) Are there any other reasons that have led to this event?

Act 3, Scene 2

Juliet waits for Romeo to arrive to celebrate their marriage. She is excited at the prospect and totally unprepared for the tragic news of Tybalt's death brought to her by the Nurse. The drama is heightened by the confused presentation of the news about who is dead and who is responsible.

Activity 18

Juliet's feelings change rapidly in this scene. Below are some line beginnings to track through the scene. Describe Juliet's thoughts and feelings and how they change at each given point.

a) 'Gallop apace, you fiery-footed steeds...'

---

b) 'Now, Nurse, what news?...'

---

c) 'Can heaven be so envious?'

---

d) 'I am not I, if there be such an "ay"...'

---

e) 'What storm is this that blows so contrary?...'

---

f) 'O God, did Romeo's hand shed Tybalt's blood?'

----

g) 'Beautiful tyrant, fiend angelical!...'

----

h) 'Blister'd be thy tongue...'

----

i) 'Will you speak well of him that killed your cousin?...'

----

j) '"Romeo is banished": to speak that word...'

----

k) 'But I, a maid, die maiden-widowed...'

Act 3, Scene 3

Realising that he has caused more problems by marrying Romeo and Juliet, despite his good intentions, Friar Lawrence advises Romeo that it would be better to accept his punishment than risk death.

> **Key quotations**
>
> 'There is no world without Verona walls,
> But purgatory, torture, hell itself:' *(Romeo)*

Activity 19

Explore how the plot develops in this scene by answering the following questions. Add brief textual evidence to support your ideas.

a) Why does Romeo feel that the prospect of the Prince's sentence of banishment from Verona **'hath more terror'** than death?

----

b) Other than to save Romeo's life, why might Friar Lawrence be so keen for Romeo to accept the Prince's punishment?

----

c) In his speech beginning **'Hold thy desperate hand!'**, Friar Lawrence persuades Romeo that killing himself is not the answer. Summarise his argument.

Act 3, Scene 4

Lord and Lady Capulet talk with Paris about his planned marriage to Juliet.

> **Key quotations**
>
> ''Tis very late, she'll not come down tonight.' *(Lord Capulet)*
>
> 'A'Thursday let it be – a'Thursday, tell her,
> She shall be married to this noble earl.' *(Lord Capulet)*

Activity 20

a) What do you think this scene demonstrates about the role of Lady Capulet in helping to decide her daughter's future at this point?

----

b) Circle the word(s) you feel best characterise Lady Capulet's feelings about the proposed marriage.

caring   excited   thoughtful   maternal

enthusiastic

insensitive

indifferent

unemotional

cold   resigned   powerless

Act 3, Scene 5

In the second half of this scene Lord Capulet orders his daughter to marry Paris or face banishment from the family. Juliet realises that she can no longer rely on the Nurse for help and support, as she advises Juliet to forget Romeo and marry Paris.

> **Key quotations**
>
> 'I must be gone and live, or stay and die.' *(Romeo)*
>
> 'O think'st thou we shall ever meet again?' *(Juliet)*
>
> 'Do as thou wilt, for I have done with thee.' *(Lady Capulet)*

Activity 21

a) Explore the way that the characters will be thinking about the events in this scene. We know what Juliet thinks about the Nurse, but what is the Nurse thinking? Juliet's perspective of this has been completed for you to reflect what is said by Juliet after the Nurse has left the scene. Do the same for Juliet and both Lady Capulet (below) and Lord Capulet (on page 24).

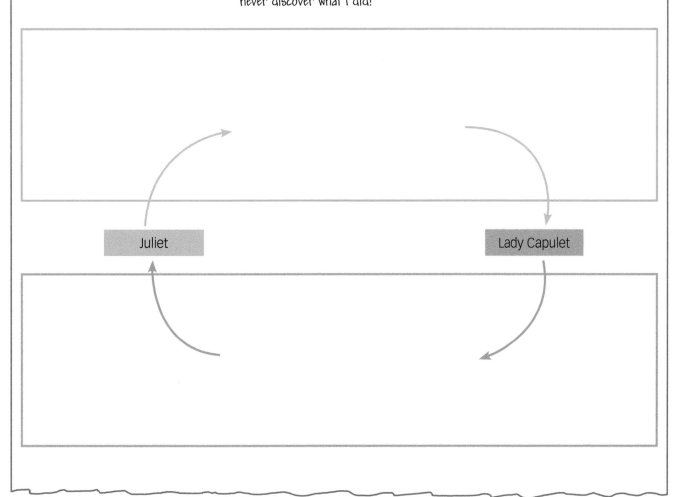

I can never trust your word again. You have let me down and I cannot share my thoughts with you as I have always done since I was a child. I only have Romeo to rely on now, but cannot reach him. I am in despair!

Juliet

Nurse

Oh I hope everything is going to work out well now. My mistress seemed to agree that she should forget Romeo and look forward to a life with Paris. I hope my Lord and Lady never discover what I did!

Juliet

Lady Capulet

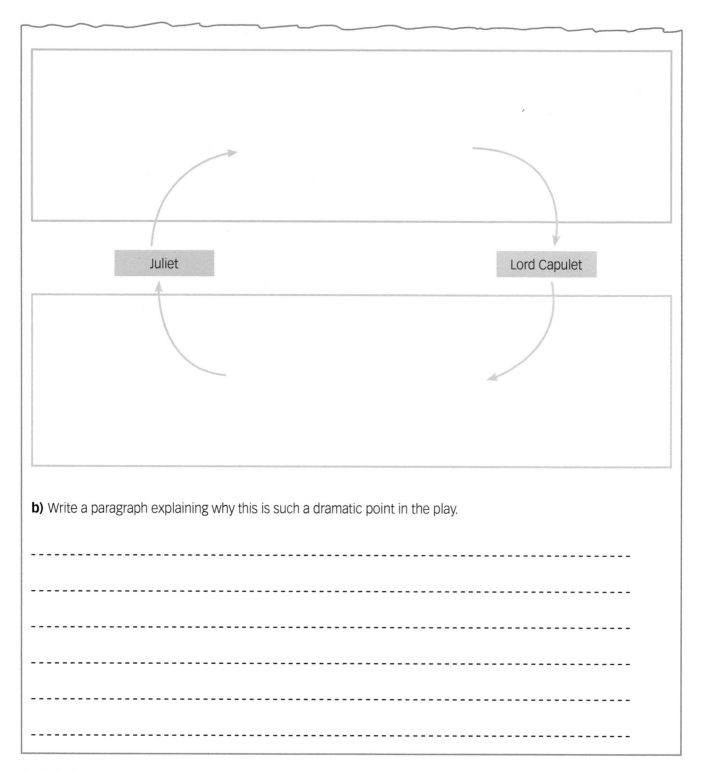

Juliet

Lord Capulet

b) Write a paragraph explaining why this is such a dramatic point in the play.

Act 4, Scene 1

Paris is speaking to Friar Lawrence about the impending marriage and briefly talks to Juliet before leaving. Her responses are full of **dramatic irony**. Friar Lawrence now replaces the Nurse as Juliet's confidant as they plan a way out of her marriage to Paris.

> **dramatic irony** when the words or action of a scene are understood by the audience, but not by one or more of the characters on stage – leading to a greater sense of involvement and anticipation

Key quotations

'O bid me leap, rather than marry Paris,
From off the battlements of any tower,' *(Juliet)*

'No warmth, no breath shall testify thou livest;' *(Friar Lawrence)*

Activity 22

Romeo threatened to kill himself while outlining his dilemma with Friar Lawrence in Act 3, Scene 3, but Juliet is equally desperate. She has to decide between marrying Paris or drinking a potion to make it appear as if she were dead.

Consider the consequences of Juliet's possible options, remembering to look back at other scenes in the play.

If she marries Paris	If she drinks the potion
1 She will break God's law and go against the Church by committing bigamy (marrying twice)	1 She may be the victim of a trick – Friar Lawrence may be scared of being uncovered and wishes her dead
2 ------------------------------- ------------------------------- -------------------------------	2 ------------------------------- ------------------------------- -------------------------------
3 ------------------------------- ------------------------------- -------------------------------	3 ------------------------------- ------------------------------- -------------------------------
4 ------------------------------- ------------------------------- -------------------------------	4 ------------------------------- ------------------------------- -------------------------------

Act 4, Scene 2

Juliet's father is surprised and pleased to see an apologetic Juliet agree to the marriage with Paris. He accelerates the wedding day to Wednesday, though Lady Capulet argues against this alteration.

> **Key quotations**
>
> 'My heart is wondrous light,
> Since this same wayward girl is so reclaim'd.' *(Lord Capulet)*

Act 4, Scene 3

During this scene the audience witnesses the extremes of the dilemma faced by Juliet. She has an internal debate as to whether or not to take the potion.

> **Key quotations**
>
> 'What if this mixture do not work at all?
> Shall I be married then tomorrow morning?' *(Juliet)*
>
> 'Romeo, Romeo, Romeo! Here's drink – I drink to thee.' *(Juliet)*

Activity 23

At this point, Juliet knows that she will either die or wake at the planned time and meet her husband again. She also knows that she will never see her family again. Write a letter as Juliet, explaining all the feelings that she would want her family to know – with the assumption that it was meant to be read before she married Paris. You may wish to consider the prompts below.

- How might Juliet feel about her parents – does she love or respect them? Was Paris a good suitor for her?
- What were her parents' motivations? What did they ultimately want for Juliet?
- What part has the Nurse played in Juliet's life?
- Remember to look at what Juliet *says* in the play to her family to guide your interpretation of her feelings.

My Dear Lord and Father

Act 4, Scene 4

In this short scene, the household prepares for the wedding while the audience waits for Juliet to be discovered. Lord Capulet's joy and enthusiasm at the preparations fill the short scene with dramatic irony.

> **Key quotations**
>
> 'Go waken Juliet, go and trim her up,
> I'll go and chat with Paris.' *(Lord Capulet)*

Act 4, Scene 5

The dramatic irony continues until it is realised by the family that Juliet is 'dead'. Only Friar Lawrence and the audience know the truth. He tells them they should rejoice that she is in heaven. The plan has worked to this point.

> **Key quotations**
>
> 'O love! O life! not life, but love in death!' *(Paris)*

metaphor a figure of speech applied to something to suggest a resemblance, without using the words 'like' or 'as'

Activity 24

There are numerous literal and **metaphorical** references to death in this scene. Identify the references and their effect in the table below. The first two have been completed for you.

Quotation	Effect
Nurse: 'She's dead, decease'd, she's dead, alack the day!'	This announces Juliet's death and sets the scene.
Lady Capulet: 'Alack the day, she's dead, she's dead, she's dead!'	Almost a repeat of the Nurse's reaction – both reacting like mothers?

Activity 25

Why do you think that Shakespeare refers to death so much in this scene, given that the audience knows that Juliet is not really dead?

Act 5, Scene 1

Romeo's positive mood is destroyed when Balthasar brings news of Juliet's death. Romeo remains unaware of Friar Lawrence's scheme.

> **Key quotations**
>
> 'Come, cordial and not poison, go with me
> To Juliet's grave, for there must I use thee.' *(Romeo)*

Act 5, Scene 2

The scene exists to complicate the approaching tragedy further. Friar John, sent to warn Romeo that Juliet will wake from her seeming death, explains to Friar Lawrence that he was prevented from reaching him. Friar Lawrence realises that he will have to be there when Juliet awakes.

Act 5, Scene 3

This is the longest scene of the play and is punctuated by the deaths and discoveries. Romeo kills Paris outside the tomb before poisoning himself at Juliet's side. Juliet awakens just as Romeo dies and then kills herself with Romeo's dagger after not finding enough poison on his lips. The bodies are discovered, Friar Lawrence explains the whole story and the families are reconciled by the shock of the loss of their children.

> **Key quotations**
>
> 'O brother Montague, give me thy hand.
> This is my daughter's jointure, for no more
> Can I demand.' *(Lord Capulet)*

Activity 26

The scene is divided into different moments of drama. These 'moments' may signal a dramatic twist, the introduction of a new character to the scene or a development in the plot. Look again at the scene as a whole and decide where you think different sections begin (there could be anything between six and eight depending on your perspective). Use the table opposite to note your thoughts.

Section	Who is on stage?	What happens?
Beginning of the scene	Paris and Page	Paris guards the tomb, then notices Romeo's arrival

Structure

The order of events

 Activity 27

There is a clear timeline that underpins the structure of *Romeo and Juliet*. The play contains some explicit references to time and different characters' plans for the future. The action takes place between the Sunday morning and Thursday evening of a single week. Use the table below to track some of the references. You can create a more detailed list by adding to those listed here on separate paper if you wish.

Reference to time	Point in the play	Effect
'two hours' traffic'	The Prologue	The Chorus prepares the audience for a specific length of performance
'Many a morning hath he there been seen'	Act 1, Scene 1	Emphasises that this love sickness has lasted a while
'Let two more summers wither in their pride'	Act 1, Scene 2	
'By the hour of nine'	Act 2, Scene 2	
'three-hours wife'	Act 3, Scene 2	

Activity 28

Number these soliloquies so that they are in the correct sequence according to when they occur in the play.

Juliet – impatiently waiting for the Nurse   - - - - - - -

Romeo – realising he has killed Paris   - - - - - - -

Romeo – stunned by Juliet's beauty   - - - - - - -

Romeo – waking from a happy dream   - - - - - - -

Juliet – realising that she is in love with Romeo   - - - - - - -

Friar Lawrence – describing the good and bad in nature   - - - - - - -

Juliet – realising that Romeo is dead   - - - - - - -

Juliet – impatiently waiting for Romeo   - - - - - - -

Romeo – looking at Juliet's apparent corpse   - - - - - - -

Romeo – planning to rejoin Juliet   - - - - - - -

Juliet – debating whether to take the potion   - - - - - - -

Romeo – listening to Juliet late at night   - - - - - - -

Getting an overview

Take care not to retell events from the play without careful selection. It is very easy to fall into the trap of 'telling the story' of the play. You can help develop your ability to select events for inclusion in an answer in the examination by:

- keeping a brief summary of the main events
- using a list of key quotations to trigger your memory
- colour coding notes so that you can see, for example, how often characters appear.

In this way you will have a clear overview of the play by the time you take the examination.

Activity 29

The following table contains descriptions of key events in the play. Number them in chronological order. Comment on their significance to the plot.

Event	Order	Significance
Tybalt dies at the hands of Romeo		From this point, Romeo is seen as a criminal by the law of Verona.
Romeo learns that Juliet has died		
Romeo's parents are worried about him		
Lord Capulet orders Juliet to marry Paris		
Romeo and Juliet talk to each other about their love after the ball		
Romeo and Juliet fall in love at first sight		
Juliet takes the potion given to her by Friar Lawrence		

Progress check

Use the chart below to review the skills you have developed in this chapter.
For each column, start at the bottom box and work your way up towards the highest level in the top box. Tick the box to show you have achieved that level.

Personal response	Language, structure, form	Textual references
I can sustain a critical response to *Romeo and Juliet* and interpret the plot and structure convincingly ☐	I can analyse the effects of Shakespeare's use of language, structure and form in *Romeo and Juliet*, using subject terms judiciously ☐	I can use well-integrated textual references from *Romeo and Juliet* to support my interpretation ☐
I can develop a coherent response to *Romeo and Juliet* and explain the plot and structure clearly ☐	I can explain how Shakespeare uses language, structure and form to create effects in *Romeo and Juliet*, using relevant subject terms ☐	I can use quotations and other textual references from *Romeo and Juliet* to support my explanation ☐
I can make some comments on the plot and structure in *Romeo and Juliet* ☐	I can identify some of Shakespeare's methods in *Romeo and Juliet* and use some subject terms ☐	I can make references to some details from *Romeo and Juliet* ☐

Context

Shakespeare in time

What is the effect of his life and works?

- The plays and poetry of William Shakespeare are still read and performed all over the world, almost 400 years after the publication of the First Folio of his works in 1623.
- His name is recognised worldwide and is associated with literary quality and heritage.
- His works are studied in virtually all schools and universities for exams.
- Shakespeare has become a cultural icon.
- His grave is visited by many thousands of tourists every year and he is commemorated in Poets' Corner in Westminster Abbey.

> **patriarchy/ patriarchal** a system or society based on the dominance of men over women

Activity 1

Every writer reflects the historical and cultural context in which they lived through the subject matter, references and language of their works. The table below lists aspects of life in the 16th Century. Where are they reflected in *Romeo and Juliet*? The first one has been completed for you.

Aspects of life	Where in the play?
It was illegal to sell deadly poisons to the general public.	Romeo bribes the Apothecary to obtain the poison he needs to commit suicide. He is told that it is against 'Mantua's law' to sell it. (Act 5, Scene 1)
Medicines were not commercially made or generally available.	
Wives were expected to obey the demands of their husbands.	
There were formal methods of settling arguments through fighting by rules.	
Drastic measures had to be taken to control the spread of illnesses.	
You did not always marry someone you loved.	
Virtually everyone believed in God.	
Daughters were viewed as the property of their fathers.	
Many children did not survive childbirth or died very young.	
People could be executed for breaking the law.	
Wealthy mothers paid others to breastfeed their children.	

Activity 2

Write a paragraph explaining how much choice of partner for marriage Juliet has in a society governed by **patriarchy**. You should consider:

- the role played by Lady Capulet and the Nurse as well as Lord Capulet
- the way that Shakespeare presents the marriage plans
- whether Juliet is presented as a possession to be sold or a person with her own feelings.

Use the quotations below to support your ideas and find others in the scenes to develop your answer.

> **Key quotations**
>
> 'Let two more summers wither in their pride,
> Ere we may think her ripe to be a bride.'
> *(Lord Capulet to Paris – Act 1, Scene 2)*
>
> 'Thus then in brief:
> The valiant Paris seeks you for his love.'
>
> *(Lady Capulet to Juliet – Act 1, Scene 3)*
>
> 'Nay, he's a flower, in faith, a very flower.'
>
> *(Nurse to Juliet – Act 1, Scene 3)*

Religion played a very important role in the everyday lives of people in the 16th century. The power of the Church was second only to the monarch (or equal – depending on your perspective). The Elizabethan audience believed the monarch was chosen by God, and in a Protestant England this also made the monarch head of the Church. Although set in Catholic Italy, the play clearly reflects the familiar power of the Church, and the role of a priest in people's lives.

Activity 3

Explore the way that religion influences the events of the play.

You could note your thoughts in a series of key points, as in the table below, and make more detailed notes based on these points.

Aspect of religion	Influence in the play
A priest is an important character	He marries Romeo and Juliet in secret, helps Romeo escape and Juliet appear dead.
Prayers	
Role of marriage	
References to God	
References to Church	

Sources for *Romeo and Juliet*

Plays written in the Elizabethan period frequently used a story already in existence with which their audience might be familiar. It was not something playwrights were criticised for doing. Writers wrote plays that they knew would be crowd-pleasers and the copyright laws of the day did not prevent plots being copied. Authorities used their powers to check that texts did not contain anti-monarchy or anti-religious thinking. Shakespeare would almost certainly have been familiar with a long poem by the writer Arthur Brooke called *The Tragicall Historye of Romeus and Juliet*. Published in 1562, it was the first version of the story written in English.

Activity 4

Below are some quotations from the poem by Arthur Brooke. Say in each case how Shakespeare treats that aspect of the plot or character. In what way, if any, is his treatment different? The first one has been done for you.

Quotation from the poem	Shakespeare's treatment
'They wed in shrift by counsel of a friar. Young Romeus climbs fair Juliet's bower by night. Three months he doth enjoy his chief delight.'	Although the marriage by the friar is the same, the 'three months' is shortened to one night.
'Her husband hears the tidings of her death. He drinks his bane. And she with Romeus' knife, When she awakes, herself, alas! she slay'th.'	
'So stern she was of cheer, for all the pain he took, That, in reward of toil, she would not give a friendly look.'	
"Wherefore henceforth I will far from her take my flight; Perhaps mine eye once banished by absence from her sight,"	
'Such was among the bashful maids Mercutio to behold. With friendly gripe he seized fair Juliet's snowish hand:'	
"No, coward, traitor boy," quoth he, "straightway I mind to try, Whether thy sugared talk, and tongue so smoothly filed, Against the force of this my sword shall serve thee for a shield." *(The speaker is Tybalt)*	
'Scarce saw she yet full sixteen years: too young to be a bride!'	
"Take fifty crowns of gold," quoth he, "give them thee, So that, before I part from hence, thou straight deliver me Some poison strong,"	

Activity 5

Shakespeare used many names, plot developments and ideas from Brooke's poem to create his own play *Romeo and Juliet*.

How far do you agree with the following statement: 'Shakespeare did not really create his own play but copied Brooke's poem'? Use your answers to Activity 4 as evidence.

Links to modern thinking

A character in Jane Austen's novel *Mansfield Park*, written in the 18th century, says:

> 'No doubt one is familiar with Shakespeare in a degree… from one's earliest years. His celebrated passages are quoted by everybody; they are in half the books we open, and we all talk Shakespeare, use his similes, and describe with his descriptions'.

Although there is much that is different between our world and the time of Shakespeare, it should be seen as an exciting time of change. The theatre played a part in helping to make those changes, especially in the way people thought about the issues of the day or the past. Shakespeare was constantly inventive in his language and there are many expressions from *Romeo and Juliet* that we hear and use today.

> **Upgrade**
>
> Contextual information is *only useful* to include in an exam answer if it is *directly relevant* to the point you are making. A brief reference to Shakespeare's creativity with language might be appropriate but an examiner would not expect you then to explain all the words Shakespeare created, or list those we use today.

Activity 6

Look at the following phrases from *Romeo and Juliet*. See if you can remember when they are used in the play.

"past hope"	"last embrace"	"in a fool's paradise"	"what must be shall be"
"what's in a name?"	"above compare"	"last farewell"	"let me alone"
"as gentle as a lamb"	"in one short minute"	"on a wild goose chase"	"past help"
"fortune's fool"	"born to die"	"go like lightning"	"on pain of death"
"stiff and stark"	"light of heart"	"I will not budge"	"I thought all for the best"

Select five of these words and phrases and explain how they would be used in a modern context.

a) --

----

b) --

----

c) --

----

d) --

----

e) --

Progress check

Use the chart below to review the skills you have developed in this chapter.
For each column, start at the bottom box and work your way up towards the
highest level in the top box. Tick the box to show you have achieved that level.

I can use well-integrated textual references from *Romeo and Juliet* to support my interpretation ☐	I can show a perceptive understanding of how *Romeo and Juliet* is shaped by its context ☐
I can use quotations and other textual references from *Romeo and Juliet* to support my explanation ☐	I understand the context of *Romeo and Juliet* and can make connections between the text and its context ☐
I can make references to some details from *Romeo and Juliet* ☐	I am aware of the context in which *Romeo and Juliet* was written ☐
Textual references	**Text and context**

Characters

Main Characters

Romeo

One of the two **eponymous** protagonists, Romeo is introduced in the first scene as someone who has been noticed as acting strangely by his friends and family. The reason for his behaviour – the pain of his unrequited (unreturned) love – is soon replaced by the joy of meeting Juliet.

eponymous referring to the fact that the character's name forms part of the title of the play

> **Key quotations**
>
> 'In sadness, cousin, I do love a woman.' *(Romeo, Act 1, Scene 1)*
>
> 'O she doth teach the torches to burn bright!' *(Romeo, Act 1, Scene 5)*

Activity 1

To the point in the play (Act 1, Scene 5) where Romeo has fallen in love with Juliet, Romeo has been presented as a lost soul, a lovesick teenager, someone who is reluctant to talk to his friends and who has to be almost bullied into attending the Capulets' party.

Write a paragraph that:

- explains how he is described by others before he appears on stage
- describes his behaviour in Act 1 up to the party
- shows how his character changes when he sees Juliet.

Include short quotations in your answer to support your points.

Activity 2

a) Romeo describes his feelings of love on many occasions in the play. Find some more examples and complete the table below.

Act/Scene	Quotation	Significance
Act 1, Scene 1: Romeo describes the pain of love to Benvolio	'This love feel I, that feel no love in this. / Dost thou not laugh?'	He is aware that there has been a brawl but is still heavily affected by his love-sickness
Act 1, Scene 1: Romeo explains Rosaline's rejection	'she'll not be hit/ With Cupid's arrow, she hath Dian's wit;'	He is powerless to make Rosaline return his love for her

b) 'Romeo has a consistent attitude to love throughout *Romeo and Juliet*.' Write a paragraph saying whether you agree with this statement, using some of the evidence you have collected.

Romeo is not always presented as a joyful lover. He also has the potential for aggression and self-destruction. This aspect of his character is triggered by rage and despair, especially when he has lost control of his own destiny.

 Activity 3

Complete the table below by finding where the moment occurs, recounting what is said, or explaining what the moment shows about Romeo at this point in the play.

Act/Scene	Quotation	What it shows
Act 3, Scene 1	'And fire-ey'd fury be my conduct now!'	Romeo has done his best to avoid conflict, but his friend's death makes him lose control.
	'O, I am fortune's fool.'	Romeo realises that his actions will have terrible consequences.
Act 3, Scene 3	'O Friar, the damned use that word in hell; / Howling attends it.'	
Act 3, Scene 3		He is desperate to hear how Juliet is feeling, assuming that their future together is over.
	'Is it e'en so? then I defy you, stars!'	
Act 5, Scene 1		He demands that the Apothecary sell him poison, when refused.
Act 5, Scene 3	'The time and my intents are savage-wild,'	

Juliet

The character of Juliet is presented as a strong, individual young woman; a match for Romeo in more ways than one. However, like her mother and the Nurse, she is under the control of the narrow patriarchal world of the Capulet household. She is loyal to her family, but willing to give up her security and reputation – and her life – for the love of Romeo.

Key quotations

'Madam, I am here, what is your will?' *(Juliet, Act 1, Scene 3)*

'O bid me leap, rather than marry Paris, / From off the battlements of any tower,' *(Juliet, Act 4, Scene 1)*

Activity 4

The character of Juliet is presented as a thoughtful and emotional individual throughout the play. Complete the spider diagram below by selecting quotations from the text to demonstrate each aspect of her character.

Activity 5

Compose a suitable **epitaph** for Juliet that will appear on a social media site. You are restricted to 50 words so will need to focus on what made her so memorable. Clearly, she died a needless and tragic death, so think carefully about what needs to be written to help others learn – both old and young.

Nurse

The Nurse has been a second mother to Juliet throughout her life. She is able to reminisce about her early childhood in Act 1, Scene 3 when Juliet's actual mother has little to add. She is the go-between who passes messages between the two lovers and enjoys teasing Juliet. She is presented as a confident woman who stands up for herself against Mercutio's rudeness.

epitaph a short text honouring someone who has died, sometimes expressing a message, moral or warning

Key quotations

'Then hie you hence to Friar Lawrence' cell,
There stays a husband to make you a wife.' *(Nurse, Act 2, Scene 5)*

'I think it best you married with the County.' *(Nurse, Act 3, Scene 5)*

Look at the extract opposite from Act 3, Scene 5. The Nurse has to change her behaviour in this scene as Juliet faces the anger of her father when she declines to follow his wishes and marry Paris.

Activity 6

Create some stage directions for the extract that show how you feel the Nurse might show her reaction through facial expression, tone of voice, gestures and use of space on stage in relation to the other characters. An example has been done for you.

Lady Capulet

Ay, sir; but she will none, she gives you thanks.
I would the fool were married to her grave!

Capulet

Soft, take me with you, take me with you, wife.
How, will she none? doth she not give us thanks?
Is she not proud? doth she not count her blest,
Unworthy as she is, that we have wrought
So worthy a gentleman to be her bridegroom?

Juliet

Not proud, you have, but thankful, that you have:
Proud can I never be of what I hate,
But thankful even for hate that is meant love.

Capulet

How now, how how, chopt-logic? What is this?
'Proud,' and 'I thank you,' and 'I thank you not',
And yet 'not proud,' mistress minion you?
Thank me no thankings, nor, proud me no prouds,
But fettle your fine joints 'gainst Thursday next,
To go with Paris to Saint Peter's Church,
Or I will drag thee on a hurdle thither.
Out, you green-sickness carrion! out, you baggage!
You tallow-face!

Lady Capulet

Fie, fie! what, are you mad?

Juliet

Good father, I beseech you on my knees,
Hear me with patience but to speak a word.

Capulet

Hang thee, young baggage, disobedient wretch!
I tell thee what: get thee to church a'Thursday,
Or never after look me in the face.
Speak not, reply not, do not answer me!
My fingers itch. Wife, we scarce thought us blest
That God had lent us but this only child,
But now I see this one is one too much,
And that we have a curse in having her.
Out on her, hilding!

Nurse

God in heaven bless her!
You are to blame, my lord, to rate her so.

The Nurse is worried and looks from Lady Capulet to her husband

43

Activity 7

At the end of the play Friar Lawrence admits to his role in bringing the two lovers together. The Nurse is not formally present at this scene in the text but she is named by the Friar as knowing of the secret love; almost certainly she would be questioned afterwards.

Write the Nurse's account/confession of her role in the tragedy for an enquiry into the deaths of the lovers. Help her to explain that she thought she was acting in the best interests of Juliet. Will she regret what she has done? You may wish to include:

- some form of apology

- some memories of Juliet's childhood

- why she was overcome with the romance of the situation

- why she did not tell Juliet's parents

- what she wishes she had done.

Friar Lawrence

Friar Lawrence acts as Romeo's confidant and marries the young couple in an attempt to bring the families together. At the end of the play he explains what he did to the gathering around the bodies of Romeo and Juliet.

> **Key quotations**
>
> 'Young men's love then lies
> Not truly in their hearts, but in their eyes.'
> *(Friar Lawrence, Act 2, Scene 3)*
>
> 'For this alliance may so happy prove
> To turn your households' rancour to pure love.'
> *(Friar Lawrence, Act 2, Scene 3)*

At the end of the play, Prince Escales publicly forgives Friar Lawrence for what he has done: **'We still have known thee for a holy man'** *(Act 5, Scene 3)*. He acknowledges that the Friar would not have acted out of malice as he is a man of the Church. However, it is possible to view the Friar's behaviour in the play as reckless.

Activity 8

Use the following table to consider the motivation of Friar Lawrence at each decision he makes.

Decision	Motivation
He decides to help Romeo	He can see that Romeo is in a desperate state. He also feels that he may be able to heal the rift between the families.
He marries the couple	
He talks Romeo out of suicide	
He sends Romeo to spend the night with Juliet	
He decides on the sleeping potion scheme	

Activity 9

Imagine that a court case has been brought to judge Friar Lawrence's role in the deaths of the two young people. Fill in the table below to present evidence first for the prosecution (those trying to convince a court of a person's guilt) and then for the defence (those trying to convince a court of a person's innocence).

Friar Lawrence	
Guilty	**Innocent**
He did not warn the families that the young people were in love.	He was conscious of his role as a confidant and keeping Romeo's trust.

Tybalt

Juliet's cousin is presented as an angry young man, who enjoys the family feud and looks to fight at any opportunity. He challenges Romeo and kills Mercutio instead of ignoring him.

> **Key quotations**
>
> 'What, drawn and talk of peace? I hate the word,
>
> As I hate hell, all Montagues, and thee.' *(Tybalt, Act 1, Scene 1)*

Activity 10

Write your thoughts about why Tybalt is so quick to fight, considering each of the following points:

a) his reputation, e.g. Act 3, Scene 1

----

b) what is said about him, e.g. Act 1, Scene 5

----

c) the rules of honour, e.g. Act 3, Scene 1

----

d) his role in the family hierarchy, e.g. Act 1, Scene 5.

Benvolio

Benvolio, Romeo's friend, is presented as a peacemaker, someone who avoids conflict and is acutely aware of the Prince's warning about fighting in the streets. He is presented as being able to show empathy towards others, and is the calm **antithesis** to Tybalt.

antithesis a person or thing that is the direct opposite of another

> **Key quotations**
>
> 'Part, fools!
> Put up your swords, you know not what you do.' *(Benvolio, Act 1, Scene 1)*
>
> 'And if we meet we shall not scape a brawl,
> For now, these hot days, is the mad blood stirring.' *(Benvolio, Act 3, Scene 1)*

Activity 11

On separate paper, complete the spider diagram to record evidence of where Benvolio acts in the interests of others rather than himself.

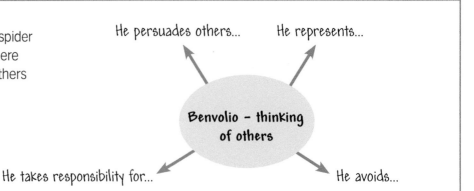

He persuades others...

He represents...

Benvolio – thinking of others

He takes responsibility for...

He avoids...

Mercutio

Mercutio is an intriguing character whose fast-paced humour is the perfect device to shake Romeo out of his mood. Being a member of the family of Prince Escales, Mercutio's death increases the tragedy of Verona. His cry of **'A plague a' both houses!'** *(Act 3, Scene 1)* and very public death is a key turning point in the plot and significantly alters the mood of the play.

> **Key quotations**
>
> 'now art thou Romeo; now art thou what thou art, by art as well as by nature,' *(Mercutio, Act 2, Scene 4)*
>
> 'O calm, dishonourable, vile submission!' *(Mercutio, Act 3, Scene 1)*

Activity 12

If you were a theatre director, what qualities would you need in the actor playing Mercutio? Imagine a director has decided to search for an actor using an advert. Write the description of the skills needed by the actor who is to play Mercutio. You should include references to the play to explain the qualities needed.

Attention – looking for Mercutio!

Lord Capulet

Lord Capulet cares for his daughter but is consumed with rage when Juliet initially refuses the marriage with Paris. He is a dominant patriarch and a loving father, a difficult combination. He has the sense to make peace with Lord Montague at the end of the play.

> **Key quotations**
>
> 'My child is yet a stranger in the world,
> She hath not seen the change of fourteen years;' *(Lord Capulet, Act 1, Scene 2)*
>
> 'Am I the master here, or you? go to!' *(Lord Capulet, Act 1, Scene 5)*

Activity 13

a) Comment on the behaviour of Lord Capulet towards his daughter, his wife and the Nurse in the play. Use short quotations to support your thoughts.

i. Lord Capulet and Juliet:

----

ii. Lord Capulet and Lady Capulet:

----

iii. Lord Capulet and the Nurse:

----

b) Based on what you have learned about Lord Capulet, explain two aspects of his behaviour that would be unacceptable from a modern perspective. Use short, integrated quotations to support your thoughts.

Lady Capulet

Juliet's mother was married to her husband at a young age and this may explain why she is not strongly against her daughter's proposed marriage to Paris. She voices some opinions and can react quite aggressively, such as her demand that Romeo be executed after killing Tybalt. However, within the patriarchal system she is unable to speak openly against her husband because he will always have the ultimate authority: she will always be subservient or less important. She can be seen to be emotionally distant from her daughter when compared to the careful nurturing of the Nurse, though she is clearly distraught at Juliet's apparent death.

> **Key quotations**
>
> 'Prince, as thou art true,
> For blood of ours, shed blood of Montague' *(Lady Capulet, Act 3, Scene 1)*
>
> 'O me, O me, my child, my only life!
> Revive, look up, or I will die with thee.' *(Lady Capulet, Act 4, Scene 5)*

Activity 14

By understanding more of the context of Lady Capulet's world and the subservient role of women in the time the play is set, it is possible to sympathise with her apparent lack of empathy.

In your opinion, can all her behaviour towards her daughter be understood when seen in the context of the time? Explain your thoughts using short, integrated quotations to support your ideas.

Lady Capulet – can we sympathise?

Lord and Lady Montague

The parents of Romeo are less well defined than the Capulets in that we do not witness any of their domestic life in the play and only see them in public at moments of conflict or tragedy.

> **Key quotations**
>
> 'Thou shalt not stir one foot to seek a foe.' *(Lady Montague, Act 1, Scene 1)*
>
> 'Could we but learn from whence his sorrows grow,
> We would as willingly give cure as know.' *(Lord Montague, Act 1, Scene 1)*

Activity 15

Why do you think Shakespeare decided to focus less on the Montagues and more on the Capulets in the play? You could think about:

- what purposes Lord and Lady Capulet serve in the play
- the advantages and disadvantages of more focus on Lord and Lady Montague.

> **Upgrade**
>
> No character is included by accident within a play. Exam questions about character expect you to consider a character's purpose or function when you are writing about the part they play; remember also that this function may change throughout the play.

Prince Escales

Prince Escales is the only character the families listen to because he has ultimate authority in Verona. He warns the families not to fight **'on pain of death'** *(Act 1, Scene 1)* but is wise enough to exile Romeo later in the play when he hears the full details of Tybalt's death from Benvolio (even though Mercutio, a member of his own family, has been killed). It is his authoritative voice that ends the play.

> **Key quotations**
>
> 'On pain of torture, from those bloody hands
> Throw your mistemper'd weapons to the ground,' *(Prince Escales, Act 1, Scene 1)*

Activity 16

On a separate piece of paper, write a paragraph describing the overall function of Prince Escales in the play.

Paris

Paris wishes to marry Juliet and persuades her father to allow it. Paris is presented as a sincere and thoughtful young man who genuinely loves Juliet. Paris dies when killed by the desperate Romeo in the final scene. Romeo acknowledges his dying wish of being placed in Juliet's tomb before taking his own life.

> **Key quotations**
>
> 'Sweet flower, with flowers thy bridal bed I strew – / O woe, thy canopy is dust and stones! – / Which with sweet water nightly I will dew,'
> *(Paris, Act 5, Scene 3)*

Activity 17

a) Compare the way that Paris is described by Lady Capulet and the Nurse in Act 1, Scene 3 with the way Romeo is described by the Nurse in Act 2, Scene 5. Look for the key parts of the text that describe them from the perspective of physical attractiveness and personality.

Description of Paris in Act 1, Scene 3	Description of Romeo in Act 2, Scene 5
'valiant Paris' *(Lady Capulet)*	
'he's a man of wax' *(Nurse)*	
'Verona's summer hath not such a flower.' *(Lady Capulet)*	
'fair volume' *(Lady Capulet)*	
'precious book of love' *(Lady Capulet)*	

b) Which one is being portrayed as the more attractive prospect? _

c) Why does Juliet's mother describe Paris as she does?

_ _

_ _

d) Why do you think the Nurse is so enthusiastic in Act 2, Scene 5?

_ _

_ _

Minor characters

Activity 18

Clearly, the characters of Romeo and Juliet dominate this play. The other characters have a variety of roles in terms of how they react to or influence the chain of events that leads to the tragic suicide at the climax of the play.

Consider which characters (other than Romeo and Juliet) have the most influence through their actions on what happens by the end of the play. Remember that actions can sometimes have positive and negative effects. Gather your ideas on a separate piece of paper, considering different characters, their influence and any key evidence in support.

Progress check

Use the chart below to review the skills you have developed in this chapter. For each column, start at the bottom box and work your way up towards the highest level in the top box. Tick the box to show you have achieved that level.

I can sustain a critical response to *Romeo and Juliet* and interpret the characterization convincingly ☐	I can use well-integrated textual references from *Romeo and Juliet* to support my interpretation ☐	I use a wide range of vocabulary and can spell and punctuate consistently accurately ☐
I can develop a coherent response to *Romeo and Juliet* and explain the characterization clearly ☐	I can use quotations and other textual references from *Romeo and Juliet* to support my explanation ☐	I use a range of vocabulary and can spell and punctuate, mostly accurately ☐
I can make some comments on the characterization in *Romeo and Juliet* ☐	I can make references to some details from *Romeo and Juliet* ☐	I use a simple range of vocabulary and spell and punctuate with some accuracy ☐
▲ Personal response	▲ Textual references	▲ Technical accuracy

Language

Understanding the language of Shakespeare is important for many different types of exam questions. Knowledge of the effect of literary devices may be helpful in writing about characters and themes in *Romeo and Juliet* if the points made are clearly linked to the question.

Metaphor

The power of imagery to allow the audience's imagination to move beyond the literal is a key part of Shakespeare's skill as a dramatist. There are some vivid metaphors in the play and many characters have become memorable through the use of metaphor. Some **extended metaphors** are used where the image is developed over a speech, such as Lady Capulet's description of Paris, part of which can be seen below.

> **extended metaphor**
> a comparison between two things that runs on over several sentences or lines of a play or poem

Activity 1

Look at the two examples of metaphor given below. Find two more examples used by either Mercutio or Tybalt.

> **Key quotations**
>
> 'Read o'er the volume of young Paris' face,
> And find delight writ there with beauty's pen;' ——→ Lady Capulet describes Paris as a very expensive book at a time when owning books was rare.
> *(Lady Capulet, Act 1, Scene 3)*
>
> 'Why, he's a man of wax.' ——————→ Lady Capulet describes Paris as a faultless model of a man – and therefore a good husband!
> *(Lady Capulet, Act 1, Scene 3)*

a)
- -

- -

b)
- -

- -

Writing about language

Many students are led to believe that essays about Shakespeare and poetry in exams need to be filled with detailed analysis of language and identification of literary terms. This is not the case. Too much language analysis cannot fully answer any exam question. Always ensure that a writer's use of language is identified and explained appropriately in order to support the points made in the essay as a whole. For example, `the striking use of simile here, e.g. '…' makes the reader focus upon '…'.

Activity 2

A number of metaphors are linked to Juliet. Explain the effect of the metaphors in the table below in terms of how this creates a particular image of Juliet. The first one has been done for you.

Act/Scene and quotation	Effect
'So shows a snowy dove trooping with crows' *(Act 1, Scene 5)*	Juliet is clearly separated from the other young women at the ball as the only white bird among a flock of black crows. The use of 'snowy' focuses on her apparent purity and innocence while the choice of 'dove' suggests a peaceful nature.
'If I profane with my unworthiest hand This holy shrine...' *(Act 1, Scene 5)*	
'It is the east, and Juliet is the sun.' *(Act 2, Scene 2)*	
'Arise, fair sun, and kill the envious moon.' *(Act 2, Scene 2)*	

Activity 3

There is a great deal of metaphor related to Romeo in the play. Find and explore examples of these by completing the table below. Use the scene references and the given examples to start you off.

Act/Scene and quotation	Effect
'As is the bud bit with an envious worm Ere he can spread his sweet leaves to the air' *(Act 1, Scene 1)*	His father describes him as an unblossomed flower due to love-sickness.
'My lips two blushing pilgrims...' *(Act 1, Scene 5)*	
'O for a falc'ner's voice, To lure this tassel-gentle back again:' *(Act 2, Scene 2)*	
Act 2, Scene 4:	
Act 3, Scene 2:	

55

Activity 4

What is the overall effect of making Romeo the subject of so much imagery in the play? Consider:

- how his character is presented through the images
- which characters use imagery to describe him – and why they might do this
- the way that others are described through images that may reflect on Romeo.

Simile

Activity 5

As well as metaphor, Shakespeare uses **simile** as a tool to present his characters. Explore the text for the use of similes related to Juliet, using the spider diagram below. Think about:

- how the use of simile might produce a different effect to the use of metaphor
- whether different characters use simile to present Juliet in different ways
- the purpose of using simile to describe Juliet – what effect does it have?

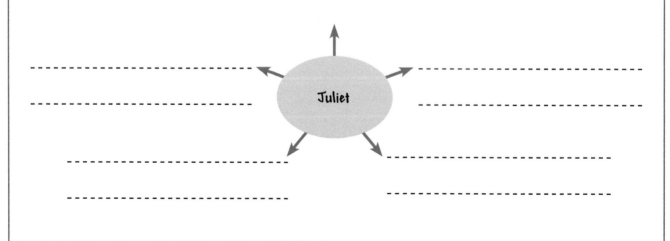

'She hangs upon the cheek of the night
Like a rich jewel in an Ethiop's ear.'
(Romeo, Act 1, Scene 5)

Romeo is dazzled by her beauty shining in the darkness

Juliet

Personification

The use of **personification** in the play gives life to certain subjects such as 'night'. It is common for the night and darkness to be referenced in Shakespeare's plays as the performances were in daylight. It was a useful dramatic device to refer constantly to the mood and the texture of the night in order to remind the audience that it was a night scene. Both metaphor and personification are used to describe the effect of night in *Romeo and Juliet*. Note the capitalisation in the following quotations that adds to the personification.

personification when human qualities are given to something non-human, such as an object or idea

simile a figure of speech applied to something to suggest a resemblance introduced by the words 'like' or 'as'

Key quotations

'Come, civil Night,
Thou sober-suited matron all in black,' *(Juliet, Act 3, Scene 2)*

'Come, gentle Night, come, loving, black brow'd Night,' *(Juliet, Act 3, Scene 2)*

Activity 6

Consider other references to night and/or darkness in the play and their effect. Use the following table to note your ideas. One has been done for you:

Quotation	Effect
'It seems she hangs upon the cheek of night' *(Act 1, Scene 5)*	
'Come, he hath hid himself among these trees / To be consorted with the humorous night:' *(Act 2, Scene 1)*	Benvolio believes that the dampness and cold of the night matches (what he still believes to be) Romeo's melancholy and lovesick nature.
'I have night's cloak to hide me from their eyes,' *(Act 2, Scene 2)*	
'The grey-ey'd morn smiles on the frowning night,' *(Act 2, Scene 3)*	
'Spread thy close curtain, love-performing Night,' *(Act 3, Scene 2)*	

Activity 7

a) Look at the extract below from Act 4, Scene 5. Highlight the references to 'dead' and 'death'.

b) Identify where you feel that personification is used as a literary device.

> **Nurse**
> She's dead, deceas'd, she's dead; alack the day!
>
> **Lady Capulet**
> Alack the day, she's dead, she's dead, she's dead!
>
> **Capulet**
> Hah, let me see her. Out alas, she's cold,
> Her blood is settled, and her joints are stiff:
> Life and these lips have long been separated;
> Death lies on her like an untimely frost
> Upon the sweetest flower of all the field.
>
> **Nurse**
> O lamentable day!
>
> **Lady Capulet**
> O woeful time!
>
> **Capulet**
> Death, that hath ta'en her hence to make me wail
> Ties up my tongue and will not let me speak.

c) Explain the effect of the different personified references to death.

Activity 8

Collect some other examples of the use of personification that you find in the play.
There are more references to 'night' and 'death' but a range of others too. Note them
in the chart below with a short explanation for each one.

Personification	Effect
'My ears have not yet drunk a hundred words Of thy tongue's uttering,' *(Juliet, Act 2, Scene 2)*	Romeo's voice is new to her, like a different taste – and yet she feels so comfortable with it.
'For exile hath more terror in his look,' *(Romeo, Act 3, Scene 3)*	Exile is a frightening prospect for Romeo – like a fearsome beast to be avoided.

Rhyming couplets

The stage convention of the Elizabethan theatre was to use verse, a heightened form of language, rather than the everyday language of the average citizen. Most of *Romeo and Juliet* is written in **blank verse**, with **rhyming couplets** used to signal moments of particular importance.

> **blank verse** unrhymed lines of poetry with regular metre
>
> **rhyming couplets** two consecutive lines that rhyme

 Activity 9

a) The following table contains some rhyming couplets from the play. Explain why each moment is significant. The first is completed for you.

Quotation	Who/Where?	Significance
'I beg for justice, which thou, Prince, must give: / Romeo slew Tybalt, Romeo must not live.'	*Lady Capulet (Act 3, Scene 1)*	She is desperate for revenge – this shows that she is part of the endless feud and wants more death.
'Hence will I to my ghostly sire's close cell, / His help to crave, and my dear hap to tell.'	*Romeo (Act 2, Scene 2)*	
'Virtue itself turns vice, being misapplied, / And vice sometime by action dignified.'	*Friar Lawrence (Act 2, Scene 3)*	
'But passion lends them power, time means, to meet, / Temp'ring extremities with extreme sweet.'	*Chorus (Act 1, Scene 5)*	
'The heavens do low'r upon you for some ill; / Move them no more by crossing their high will.'	*Friar Lawrence (Act 4, Scene 5)*	
'Compare her face with some that I shall show, / And I will make thee think thy swan a crow.'	*Benvolio (Act 1, Scene 2)*	

b) Using your notes, write a short paragraph that explains the way that the rhyming couplets signal or end particular moments in the play.

The rhythm of language

Shakespeare's verse is written in **iambic pentameter**, which means that each line has five stresses. You do not have to write in any detail about the use of iambic pentameter but it may be appropriate to mention how it works in a particular line, for example to reflect the mood of a character.

> **iambic pentameter** a line of verse with ten syllables, forming five 'feet', where the stress falls on the second syllable in each foot, e.g. 'di dum' as in 'He <u>jests</u> at <u>scars</u> that <u>never</u> <u>felt</u> a <u>wound</u>.' (Romeo, *Act 2, Scene 2*)

Activity 10

Highlight the stresses in the following lines by adding underlines. Say them aloud to feel the rhythm.

> **'Deny thy father and refuse thy name;'**
> *(Juliet, Act 2, Scene 2)*

> **'Two households, both alike in dignity.'**
> *(The Chorus, The Prologue)*

> **'Blind is his love, and best befits the dark.'**
> *(Benvolio, Act 2, Scene 1)*

> **'Thy drugs are quick. Thus with a kiss I die.'**
> *(Romeo, Act 5, Scene 3)*

You will often see contractions in the text so that a regular rhythm is consistent. This is the same process as we use in everyday speech. We contract words and phrases all the time (e.g. *do not* becomes *don't*) and signal the contraction through the apostrophe. Shakespeare's contractions do not always reflect this rule because the aim is for the rhythm to be maintained – as in **'th'inconstant moon'** (Juliet, *Act 2, Scene 2*). You will also see words that have to be pronounced differently in order to fit the rhythm of the iambic pentameter. For instance, the word **'banished'** has to be pronounced 'ban/ish/ed' by the actor playing Juliet to fit the rhythm of the lines in Act 3, Scene 3.

Activity 11

Find some other examples of contractions used in the play and words that have to be pronounced differently in order to fit the rhythm of the iambic pentameter.

Contractions	Different pronunciations

Activity 12

Sometimes an iambic line is 'shared' between two characters. The splitting of a line can often represent a sense of excitement. It has been described as the transfer of energy from one character to another. Complete the table below with some examples; one has been done for you.

Split line	Effect
Nurse: To Lammas-tide? *Lady Capulet:* A fortnight and odd days. *(Act 1, Scene 3)*	The two characters are sharing their thoughts about Juliet's age. The Nurse has been Juliet's closest companion, but Lady Capulet is her mother.

Prose

In *Romeo and Juliet*, as in other Shakespeare plays, the language of the characters who represent the lower levels of society is mostly represented through prose rather than verse.

Activity 13

Below are some examples of where prose is used in the play. Explain why you think it has been used instead of verse.

Example of prose	Why not verse?
Abram: Quarrel, sir? No, sir. *Sampson:* But if you do sir, I am for you. I serve as good a man as you. *(Act 1, Scene 1)*	
Tybalt: I am for you. [Drawing] *Romeo:* Gentle Mercutio, put thy rapier up. *Mercutio:* Come, sir, your 'passado'. *(Act 3, Scene 1)*	
Peter: You will not then? *First Musician:* No *Peter:* I will then give it you soundly. *(Act 4, Scene 5)*	

Antithesis

Shakespeare used antithesis regularly in his plays in order to reflect conflict, most often good versus evil. The underlying confusions and dilemmas faced by society or an individual character are emphasised through the **dichotomy** expressed through antithesis.

dichotomy a division or contrast between two things that are different or in opposition

Activity 14

Look for more examples of the use of antithesis in the play. Identify where you find each example and explain what you feel it represents. One has been completed for you – look for more examples from the same speech by Romeo.

Quotation	What it represents
'O brawling love, O loving hate,' *(Act 1, Scene 1)*	Romeo is so confused with his lovesick feelings for Rosaline that everything in his world seems contradictory – nothing is as it should be!

Playing with words

Shakespeare often plays with words, both for comic effect and to emphasise certain ideas and dramatic moments. Elizabethan audiences enjoyed **double entendres** and the deliberate use of **homophones** or **homographs** in **puns** to create **ambiguity** and add complexity and depth of meaning.

> **ambiguity** use of language that leaves the listener unsure of the actual meaning
>
> **double entendre** a word or phrase that is open to more than one interpretation; often used for sexual references
>
> **homograph** a word that has the same spelling and pronunciation but different meanings, e.g. *bow* (noun: a weapon used to fire arrows/the front section of a ship) and *bow* (verb: to show respect to royalty by bending forward from the waist)
>
> **homophone** a word that sounds like another with a different meaning, e.g. *stake/steak*
>
> **pun** a type of joke or word play that relies on the similar sound but different meaning of words

Activity 15

The table below lists some examples of puns from *Romeo and Juliet*. Explain the intended effect in each case, then find other examples of your own to add to the list. The first one has been done for you.

Pun	Effect
'You have dancing shoes With nimble soles, I have a soul of lead' *(Romeo, Act 1, Scene 4)*	Romeo uses the ambiguity of 'sole' (of a shoe) and 'soul' to emphasise his depression caused by his unrequited love for Rosaline.
'Give me a torch: I am not for this ambling; Being but heavy, I will bear the light.' *(Romeo, Act 1, Scene 4)*	
'That dreamers often lie. Romeo: In bed asleep, while they do dream things true.' *(Mercutio, Act 1, Scene 4)*	
'I am too sore enpierced with his shaft To soar with his light feathers,' *(Romeo, Act 1, Scene 4)*	
'Marry, that "marry" is the very theme I came to talk of.' *(Lady Capulet, Act 1, Scene 3)*	
'Hath Romeo slain himself? Say thou but "ay", And that bare vowel "I" shall poison more Than the death-darting eye of cockatrice.' *(Juliet, Act 3, Scene 2)*	

Progress check

Use the chart below to review the skills you have developed in this chapter. For each column, start at the bottom box and work your way up towards the highest level in the top box. Tick the box to show you have achieved that level.

I can analyse the effects of Shakespeare's use of language, structure and form in *Romeo and Juliet*, using subject terms judiciously ☐	I can use well-integrated textual references from *Romeo and Juliet* to support my interpretation ☐	I use a wide range of vocabulary and can spell and punctuate consistently accurately ☐
I can explain how Shakespeare uses language, structure and form to create effects in *Romeo and Juliet*, using relevant subject terms ☐	I can use quotations and other textual references from *Romeo and Juliet* to support my explanation ☐	I use a range of vocabulary and can spell and punctuate, mostly accurately ☐
I can identify some of Shakespeare's methods in *Romeo and Juliet* and use some subject terms ☐	I can make references to some details from *Romeo and Juliet* ☐	I use a simple range of vocabulary and spell and punctuate with some accuracy ☐
Language, structure, form	**Textual references**	**Technical accuracy**

Themes

Love

From its impulsive beginning to its tragic end, the dominant subject matter of the play's plot is the energy of the love between Romeo and Juliet. Their youth, which adds to the urgency of their feelings, and the way they pursue a future together in spite of the barriers that stand in their way, creates a gripping story.

What is 'love'? The play certainly offers plenty of descriptions of the way the characters feel about each other, but it is worth taking a broader view of the subject before exploring love in the play.

Activity 1

Look at the comments below:

You mean everything to me

They look good together

You make life bearable

I need you

I love him/her

She is my life

I know what she's thinking

I can't live without them

I can't think about anything else

We end each other's sentences

I worship the ground you walk on

These comments are describing different subjects of affection – some could be referring to parents, friends or even pets.

Compose your own definition of 'love' that takes into account the different ways that we can use the word to describe our feelings. Restrict yourself to 50 words.

'Love' can seem impossible to define because it means different things to different people at different times. The characters in *Romeo and Juliet* refer to love in different ways. You need to understand where these references occur as well as be able to explain how Shakespeare presents the different relationships through varying degrees of love.

Activity 2

Identify the different ways that love is demonstrated in the play by completing the following table. Find at least one example for each type of love. (Don't just think about the relationship between Romeo and Juliet!)

Description	Evidence
Concern for a child	
Loyalty to family	
Joking with a friend	
Wishing for peace	
Empathising	
Unrequited love	'Out of her favour where I am in love.' *(Romeo, Act I, Scene I)* 'She will not stay the siege of loving terms.' *(Romeo, Act I, Scene I)*
Sexual desire	
Love at first sight	

Romantic love

Shakespeare would have been very aware of the concept of romantic love. The ideal of love between a married couple was promoted strongly in society even though things may not always have gone so smoothly. For example, the relationship between Lord and Lady Capulet is not seen as particularly close from a 21st-century perspective. The love presented between Romeo and Juliet in the play perfectly captures the ideal of romantic love, shared equally between a man and a woman. The secrecy and forbidden nature of their relationship adds to its intensity.

Activity 3

Look at the quotations that refer to romantic love in the table below – the pronouns have been removed. Try to identify who is speaking and where this appears in the text.

Quotation	When?	Who?
'I have more care to stay than will to go.'		
'I will kiss thy lips,'		
'It is my _ _ _ _ _ _ _ _, O it is my love:'		
'Dost thou love me?'		
'O, _ _ _ _ _ _ _ _ is rich in beauty,'		
'Then plainly know, my heart's dear love is set'		
'_ _ _ _ _ _ _ _ is too fair, too wise, wisely too fair,'		
'My love as deep; the more I give to thee'		

Activity 4

Look again at the previous activity; the results should give you a clue as to whether it is Romeo or Juliet who more often directly describes their feelings of love in the play. Write a paragraph to explain why you think this is the case.

One aspect of romantic love is the idea of love at first sight, which supports the concept of romantic love, the discovery of a partner for life and the idea of a perfect match. The idea of the fated meeting of Romeo and Juliet is introduced in the Prologue with 'star-cross'd lovers'. The sheer thrill of the experience is powerfully presented by Shakespeare simply through the sudden change in Romeo from his depression at the impossibility of love (with Rosaline) to the joy of its new possibilities (with Juliet).

Key quotations

'Did my heart love till now?'
(Romeo, Act 1, Scene 5)

'If he be married,
My grave is like to be my wedding bed.' *(Juliet, Act 1, Scene 5)*

Activity 5

Look at the extract below, taken from the beginning of Act 2, Scene 2. Romeo has just hidden in the Capulets' orchard and is able to see Juliet at her window.

a) Annotate the text to show how Shakespeare presents Romeo's feelings. An example has been done for you.

He sees her as something dazzling and beautiful.

> *ROMEO advances*
>
> **Romeo**
>
> He jests at scars that never felt a wound.
> But soft, what light through yonder window breaks?
> It is the east, and Juliet is the sun.
> Arise, fair sun, and kill the envious moon,
> Who is already sick and pale with grief
> That thou, her maid, art far more fair than she.
> Be not her maid, since she is envious;
> Her vestal livery is but sick and green,
> And none but fools do wear it; cast it off.
>
> *JULIET appears aloft as at a window*
>
> It is my lady, O it is my love:
> O that she knew she were!
> She speaks, yet she says nothing; what of that?
> Her eye discourses, I will answer it.
> I am too bold, 'tis not to me she speaks:
> Two of the fairest stars in all the heaven,
> Having some business, do entreat her eyes,
> To twinkle in their spheres till they return.
> What if her eyes were there, they in her head?
> The brightness of her cheek would shame those stars,
> As daylight doth a lamp; her eyes in heaven
> Would through the airy region stream so bright
> That birds would sing and think it were not night.
> See how she leans her cheek upon her hand!
> O that I were a glove upon that hand,
> That I might touch that cheek!

b) Use your notes to write two paragraphs analysing how Shakespeare presents Romeo's state of mind and his changing feelings in this speech. Write your paragraphs on separate paper.

Upgrade

The thoughts and feelings of characters will not always be obviously signalled by the use of a verb such as 'I feel' or 'I think'. Emotions are often presented through other means such as the use of imagery and the asking of questions (often rhetorical).

Unrequited love

Romeo enters the play as the lovesick and vulnerable victim of unrequited love for Rosaline. He is very confused and cannot cope with the thought of a future without her.

Activity 6

Paris is also a victim of unrequited love. He is not presented as suffering as dramatically as Romeo but his sincere feelings are clear. Answer these questions to explore how Paris' feelings are presented in the play.

a) How does the audience know that Juliet does not find Paris attractive?
(*Act 1, Scene 3*)

_____

_____

b) In what ways does Paris declare his love for Juliet?
(*Act 1, Scene 2; Act 4, Scene 1; Act 5, Scene 3*)

_____

_____

_____

c) How do his actions in the final scene show the sincerity of his love?

_____

_____

Family relationships

Outside of the romantic relationships in *Romeo and Juliet*, Shakespeare explores love and loyalty within the Capulet and Montague families. There is clearly great concern for Romeo from his parents at the beginning of the play.

> **Key quotations**
>
> 'O where is Romeo? saw you him today?
> Right glad I am he was not at this fray.' (*Lady Montague, Act 1, Scene 1*)

Juliet's father seems closer to his daughter than his wife until the fateful threats in Act 3. Lady Capulet shows more emotion about the death of Tybalt until her grief at the apparent death of her daughter in Act 4.

> **Key quotations**
>
> 'Earth hath swallow'd all my hopes but she;' (*Lord Capulet, Act 1, Scene 2*)
>
> 'O me, O me, my child, my only life!
> Revive, look up, or I will die with thee.' (*Lady Capulet, Act 4, Scene 5*)

Activity 7

Look again at Act 1, Scene 2, where Lord Capulet discusses Juliet's future with Paris, and Act 3, Scene 5, where the marriage to Paris is decided.

a) What are Lord Capulet's main concerns in Act 1, Scene 2?

----

b) Does he have the same concerns at the start of his role in Act 3, Scene 5?

----

c) Why does Lady Capulet not defend her daughter in Act 3, Scene 5?

----

d) Does Lord Capulet have any choice but to react in the way he does in Act 3, Scene 5?

Activity 8

Consider the relationship between Lord and Lady Capulet and their daughter more closely. On a separate piece of paper, write an introductory paragraph to a more detailed study, highlighting the key points. Remember, the purpose of an introduction is to clearly signal your ability to select and discuss important evidence.

Conflict

Conflict, witnessed through the animosity and violence of arguments and the physical violence of the fights is a powerful theme in the play and underpins the problem of Romeo and Juliet's doomed love. Their love cuts across the divide of family loyalties and would have been seen as a betrayal of trust if it had been discovered before their deaths. Romeo and Juliet's love exists in a bubble and separates them from the hatred, fear and violence that take place around them.

Key quotations

'Is she a Capulet? / O dear account! my life is my foe's debt.'
(Romeo, Act 1, Scene 5)

'Prodigious birth of love it is to me,
That I must love a loathed enemy.' *(Juliet, Act 1, Scene 5)*

Activity 9

a) Answer the following questions, which focus on moments of conflict in the play. Use short quotations to support your ideas.

i. What was the original cause of the conflict between the Capulets and the Montagues?

----

ii. Why is it important to Sampson to **'let them begin'** the fight in Act 1, Scene 1?

----

iii. Why does Sampson say that he is not biting his thumb 'at' Abram in Act 1, Scene 1?

----

iv. Why does Lord Capulet prevent Tybalt from challenging Romeo at the party?

----

v. How does Tybalt try to provoke Romeo to fight him in Act 3, Scene 1?

----

vi. How does Lady Capulet betray her feelings of hatred in Act 3, Scene 1?

----

vii. How does Lady Capulet demonstrate her ruthlessness and hatred by what she is prepared to do for Juliet in Act 4, Scene 5?

----

b) On a separate piece of paper, write two paragraphs to answer the following question:
'How does Shakespeare use conflict to present the problems faced by the two lovers in the play?'

Different generations

The difference between the attitudes of the young and old and the need to make the most of time are important themes in the play. At the time Shakespeare wrote the play the life expectancy of the average person was far lower than it is now.

Activity 10

Look at the quotations below. All of them refer to youth, age or an attitude linked to age. Explain why the comments are important for the plot or how they develop the characters.

Quotation	What it shows
'Let two more summers wither in their pride, Ere we may think her ripe to be a bride.' (Lord Capulet, Act 1, Scene 2)	
'I was your mother much upon these years That you are now a maid.' (Lady Capulet, Act 1, Scene 3)	
'What say you, can you love the gentleman?' (Lady Capulet, Act 1, Scene 3)	
'I have seen the day That I have worn a visor and could tell A whispering tale in a fair lady's ear,' (Lord Capulet, Act 1, Scene 5)	
'Young men's love then lies Not truly in their hearts, but in their eyes.' (Friar Lawrence, Act 2, Scene 3)	

Activity 11

What difference does it make to the impact of the play that Romeo and Juliet are so young? Write your thoughts in a series of key points. One suggestion has been offered to get you started.

- They have little or no experience of life and are vulnerable to emotional reactions.

- --

- --

- --

- --

- --

- --

Friendship

Benvolio and Mercutio show different aspects of friendship in the way they relate to Romeo. For example, when attempting to shake Romeo out of his lovesickness for Rosaline, Benvolio attempts the role of counsellor, whereas Mercutio adopts merciless humour.

Activity 12

Track the ways that Benvolio and Mercutio show their friendship with Romeo in the play. Select four key moments for each and consider the effect of each on Romeo and/or the plot.

Mercutio	
Key moments of friendship with Romeo	**What is the effect?**

Benvolio	
Key moments of friendship with Romeo	**What is the effect?**

Activity 13

Who do you consider to be the better friend to Romeo? On a separate piece of paper, explain your thoughts and use short quotations to support your ideas.

Breaking the rules

The Elizabethan world was an ordered, **hierarchical** society where the power of the monarchy, the Church and the wealthy set clear limits on the 'freedom' of most people. In the play, however, many of the characters break society's rules and expectations – with varying outcomes.

> **hierarchy** a system in which there is a clear ranking of groups or individuals, some having more power and status than others

Activity 14

For each rule or expectation of behaviour in the table below, try to identify at least one example where it is broken in the play. Explain the main effect of the rule-breaking on the plot.

Rule/expectation	Where is it broken?	What is the effect?
Women are subservient to men.		
The Church only deals in spiritual matters.		
Servants obey the wishes of their employers.		
Weapons should not be used in public.		
Do not attend private family functions unless invited.		
Only God can allow you to die; you cannot take your own life.		
Children must always obey their parents.		
The dead must not be disturbed once buried or entombed.		
Bribery is a crime.		

Fate and fortune

The belief that human beings have little influence over their own destiny and that life is 'written in the stars' or in the hands of 'Lady Fortune' was common in the 16th century. A belief in fate also takes away the blame for events and puts it in the hands of an omnipotent (all-powerful) force.

Activity 15

Look at the references to fate, fortune or dreams taken from the play in the table below.

a) They are not placed in chronological order. Number them in the order they occur.

b) Identify the speaker and where the comment occurs in the play.

c) Explain why you think that fate, fortune or dreams are referenced.

Quotation	Speaker/Act/Scene	Explanation
'My dreams presage some joyful news at hand.'		
'Ay, mine own fortune in my misery.'		
'This day's black fate on more days doth depend, This begins the woe others must end.'		
'A pair of star-cross'd lovers take their life;'		
'O, I am fortune's fool.'		
'The fearful passage of their death-mark'd love,'		
'O Fortune, Fortune, all men call thee fickle;'		
'my mind misgives Some consequence yet hanging in the stars'		
'A greater power than we can contradict Hath thwarted our intents.'		
'O God, I have an ill-divining soul! Methinks I see thee now, thou art so low, As one dead in the bottom of a tomb.'		

Activity 16

Write a paragraph about the way one of the characters in the play is affected by a belief in the power of fate. Use short references to support your ideas.

 Progress check

Use the chart below to review the skills you have developed in this chapter. For each column, start at the bottom box and work your way up towards the highest level in the top box. Tick the box to show you have achieved that level.

I can sustain a critical response to *Romeo and Juliet* and interpret the themes convincingly ☐	I can use well-integrated textual references from *Romeo and Juliet* to support my interpretation ☐	I use a wide range of vocabulary and can spell and punctuate consistently accurately ☐
I can develop a coherent response to *Romeo and Juliet* and explain the themes clearly ☐	I can use quotations and other textual references from *Romeo and Juliet* to support my explanation ☐	I use a range of vocabulary and can spell and punctuate, mostly accurately ☐
I can make some comments on the themes in *Romeo and Juliet* ☐	I can make references to some details from *Romeo and Juliet* ☐	I use a simple range of vocabulary and spell and punctuate with some accuracy ☐
Personal response	**Textual references**	**Technical accuracy**

Performance

Directors and actors ('players' in the Elizabethan theatre) begin with the script of a play – the model that they then interpret to construct their performance. This leads to infinite possibilities and experiences in performances, all dependent on the space, the time, the culture, and the responses of the audience. Shakespeare was a man of the theatre and was writing with the visual and aural effect of his works at the forefront of his mind. To understand as much as possible about *Romeo and Juliet* you have to engage with the world of the play through understanding how it has been and can be performed.

Commenting on the presentation of a scene on stage highlights your understanding of the text as a drama to be performed. If possible, draw attention to **how** a moment can be dramatised by stage technique.

Script and direction

Activity 1

The stage directions in Shakespeare's plays are often very limited, sometimes just announcing the appearance and exit of characters. The table below gives some examples of stage directions from *Romeo and Juliet*. Without looking at the text, describe the moment to which each stage direction refers.

Act	Stage directions	What is happening?
1	Enter several of both houses, who join the fray,	
	They whisper in his ear	
2	Nurse calls within	
	Romeo kisses Juliet	
3	Romeo steps between them	
	Unlocks the door	
4	She kneels down	
	Draws back the curtains	
5	Gives a purse	
	Juliet rises	

Activity 2

Choose one of the stage directions in Activity 1 and add more detailed advice for an actor to make it fit your understanding of that moment. An example is given for you.

Stage direction: *'Beats down their swords'* (Act 1, Scene 1)	Stage direction:
Benvolio quickly steps in to stop the fight and is careful to focus only on the Montague servants for fear of making things worse. He speaks with authority but should show some nervousness in his eyes, hoping that the Capulet servants do not continue to fight.	

Each actor who plays a character in *Romeo and Juliet* will have to develop their own understanding of how their character will be presented to the audience. The director's guidance and interpretation of the play are also vital.

Activity 3

a) Choose one speech from any character in the play that is part of a dialogue with at least one other character. Complete the spider diagram below to help you to consider the possibilities for performing that speech.

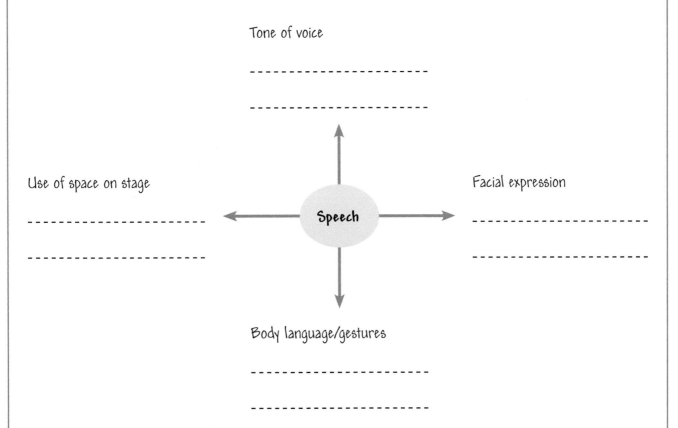

Tone of voice

- -

- -

Use of space on stage

- -

- -

Speech

Facial expression

- -

- -

Body language/gestures

- -

- -

b) In Act 2, Scene 3, the Nurse returns from meeting Romeo. She makes Juliet wait as long as possible to hear that Friar Lawrence has agreed to marry the couple. How would you direct the Nurse in this scene? Write your answer on separate paper. Use the presentational skills prompts of the spider diagram above to support your thinking.

Activity 4

Using the diagram completed for Activity 3, think about the effect of the character's performance on an audience, based on your directions.

a) How do you think the audience would feel about the character after a performance based on your ideas?

----

b) What changes could be made to the performance in order to give a different impression?

Soliloquy

An audience cannot hear the thoughts of a character so the dramatic device of soliloquy is used to voice their thoughts, often where the character is suffering some confusion or anxiety or has serious choices to make. The performance of the soliloquy is one of the most difficult for the actor as the effect needs to be dramatic without being **melodramatic**.

> **melodramatic**
> exaggerated or overemotional

Activity 5

In the play Juliet is given a number of soliloquies. Read the extract opposite from Act 2, Scene 2 and annotate it with directions to an actor who will perform it, using the presentational skills prompts from Activity 3 on page 79. Use colours to highlight specific instructions for words.

> 'Tis but thy name that is my enemy;
>
> Thou art thyself, though not a Montague.
>
> What's Montague? It is nor hand nor foot,
>
> Nor arm nor face, nor any other part
>
> Belonging to a man. O be some other name!
>
> What's in a name? That which we call a rose
>
> By any other name would smell as sweet;
>
> So Romeo would, were he not Romeo call'd,
>
> Retain that dear perfection which he owes
>
> Without that title. Romeo, doff thy name,
>
> And for thy name, which is no part of thee,
>
> Take all myself.

What do we learn from film?

You can learn a great deal about staging the play from the different filmed versions, as long as you take into account the different conventions of each media form. The full-length version of the play is rarely used for screen, and scenes may be removed or reordered. The most popular versions are those directed by Franco Zeffirelli (1968), Baz Luhrman (1996) and Carlo Carlei (2013).

A film director can concentrate the viewer's attention on a character's face using a close-up, which is not possible in the theatre. From a learning perspective this gives the chance for active and critical viewing. Scenes can be replayed, paused and analysed to develop a closer understanding of performance.

Activity 6

Look again at the soliloquy spoken by Juliet that you analysed in Activity 5.

a) Watch a filmed version of the same speech and then 'track' through the speech again, noting down how it was presented. Include:

- the film techniques used, such as zooming in
- how Juliet acts, such as gestures or physical movements
- how Juliet speaks, such as tone of voice.

b) How do these decisions help an audience understand the meaning of Juliet's soliloquy?

----

c) Compare it to your direction suggestions. Would you make any adjustments to them in light of the film direction? Why/why not?

Directors use storyboards to help visualise the way a production or film will be presented to an audience. Actors often use this technique to highlight expression and body language while rehearsing.

Activity 7

Choose eight key moments in the play that will serve to tell the story through freeze-frame images. Put them in chronological order. Describe what is seen in the image, identify the key point in the play and add a short quotation.

Image	Act/Scene	Quotation
Crossed swords held by men with angry determined faces	Prologue	'From ancient grudge break to new mutiny,'

Drama

A performance of *Romeo and Juliet* should be memorable for a powerful story told with a moral ending, warning us of the dangers of conflict and hatred. However, certain moments are more dramatic than others for a variety of reasons, for example:

- we are shocked by an event
- we are frightened
- something catches us unaware
- we feel the tension of the moment.
- we empathise with a character's emotions
- a character does something to change our view of them

You now know the play very well and have thought about it from a variety of perspectives: plot, context, characters, themes, use of language and performance.

Activity 8

Choose what you believe to be the four most dramatically effective scenes in the play. One has been completed as an example. Explain the reasons for your choice and what makes the scene so dramatic.

Dramatic moment	Reason
The death of Mercutio (Act 3, Scene 1)	Until now, Mercutio has been seen as more of a comic character. The death shocks because we know the implications for Romeo.

Progress check

Use the chart below to review the skills you have developed in this chapter. For each column, start at the bottom box and work your way up towards the highest level in the top box. Tick the box to show you have achieved that level.

Language, structure, form	Textual references	Technical accuracy
I can analyse the effects of Shakespeare's use of language, structure and form in *Romeo and Juliet*, using subject terms judiciously ☐	I can use well-integrated textual references from *Romeo and Juliet* to support my interpretation ☐	I use a wide range of vocabulary and can spell and punctuate consistently accurately ☐
I can explain how Shakespeare uses language, structure and form to create effects in *Romeo and Juliet*, using relevant subject terms ☐	I can use quotations and other textual references from *Romeo and Juliet* to support my explanation ☐	I use a range of vocabulary and can spell and punctuate, mostly accurately ☐
I can identify some of Shakespeare's methods in *Romeo and Juliet* and use some subject terms ☐	I can make references to some details from *Romeo and Juliet* ☐	I use a simple range of vocabulary and spell and punctuate with some accuracy ☐

Skills and Practice

There is no one perfect way to achieve any particular mark for an essay in your assessment. In an examination you will have to demonstrate your understanding of *Romeo and Juliet* in a limited time. However, you are more likely to write effective answers in exams if you avoid the 'Common mistakes', then try to follow the 'Things to do!' advice, both listed below.

Common mistakes

- ☒ Poor timing – too much time spent on another essay in the exam or on one particular point.
- ☒ Not answering the actual question – trying to answer one you revised instead.
- ☒ Limited personal engagement with the text and task resulting in narrative retelling of the plot.
- ☒ Limited development of ideas – points are made but not explained.
- ☒ Overuse of quotations – too many or long quotations can leave little room for expressing and developing personal ideas.
- ☒ Underuse of quotations – not enough quotation means the points made lack evidence and are less convincing.
- ☒ Overuse of technical and literary terms – knowing the terms but not linking the points made to the question or explaining the effect.

Things to do!

- ☑ Revise appropriately so that you have the necessary knowledge about plot, character, themes, context and use of language.
- ☑ Be prepared to answer different types of questions so that your knowledge is adaptable.
- ☑ Understand how to structure an answer so that your introduction is developed throughout and your conclusion sums up the important issues that you have raised.
- ☑ Use literary terms accurately and a sophisticated critical vocabulary when appropriate – especially when explaining the effects of language.
- ☑ Use short, integrated quotations accurately to support the points you make.
- ☑ Maintain a consistent viewpoint throughout.
- ☑ Write in a clear and coherent style with technical accuracy.

Effective revision techniques

Any approach to revision has to be personal and one that works for you. Some people prefer rereading notes made in class while others prefer to add new points or make new notes based on different learning. Whatever your approach, you must be prepared to give adequate time to organise yourself. Any notes you use for revision must work for you and help you to remember key points and ideas.

Plot and structure

Creating a page for each scene in the play allows you to summarise the key events from your own perspective. You could colour-code the characters who appear in each scene to track the development of their role throughout the play. Write three key things to remember in bullet points at the end of each scene. If you read the bullet points first when revising, this will be a quick reminder of events before going into more detail. Here is an example for Act 2, Scene 2:

Act 2, Scene 2 – Key Points

- Juliet declares her love for Romeo unaware that Romeo is listening.
- Romeo cannot control himself and makes his presence known to Juliet.
- They discuss their feelings and take a long time to say goodbye.

Activity 1

On separate paper, create a page for each scene in the play, like the one shown above. Add a cover sheet with one key point from each scene for even faster tracking.

It is important that you show knowledge of the whole text in your answers, whatever the specific subject identified in the question. Gaining an overview in this way helps you to 'see' the play as a whole and makes it easier to select appropriate references and events.

One way of gaining an overview is by creating a graphic image for each scene. Place the images on one sheet of paper and draw arrows between them so that you can see the chronological order.

For example, Act 1 Scene 1 could be represented like this:

Activity 2

On separate paper, design your own graphic images of each scene. You could add a key quotation or two to each image.

Character

Create a page for each character in the play. You can divide this into sections to suit you. You could use the following headings in the structure:

- Main role in the plot
- Relationships with others
- Key quotations
- Key points to remember

This approach can be adapted as you develop your learning over time. Make sure that you restrict the notes to one page for each character. As the examination approaches, this can be reduced to one flashcard so that you can carry it with you more easily.

Activity 3

On separate paper, create your own character pages for Romeo and Juliet.

Activity 4

It can be very helpful to create a diagram to represent the relationships between the characters in the play, see the example below. You may wish to think about:

- dividing the characters by family groups (Montague, Capulet, House of Escales), the three main families being represented in separate sections
- plotting characters in their order of importance either within their family or in the city of Verona
- drawing lines between the characters to represent links, with thicker lines for stronger relationships
- writing key points – perhaps quotations – to show the links in the relationship along the line.

Design your own version using whichever ideas you feel would help you.
An example is below.

Montagues: order of importance

Lord Montague

Lady Montague ———— Romeo

Benvolio

●●●● ● = friendship

Language

Activity 5

On separate paper, create a record of the different kinds of imagery used by characters throughout the play. Decide what form the record should take – table, graph, chart or graphic images. Remember to include their potential effect on an audience at that point in the play.

You could make 'language' a separate part of your character notes so that language is seen as integral or essential to that character. This will also help you to see that comments on language support questions on the presentation of themes and characters.

Upgrade

You will not be expected in an examination question to structure a whole essay around the use of language in *Romeo and Juliet*. However, you will only be able to access the highest marks by investigating some language use in your essay. For instance, if asked about Juliet's range of emotions you need to develop your points with specific comments about the effect of imagery.

Themes

Themes can be revised in a similar way. Some examples are:

- Theme headings linked to characters. For example, your page on 'Love' as a theme may include one section that notes Romeo's unrequited love for Rosaline.
- An image representing the theme could be the centre of a spider diagram or chart that enables you to make links between events and characters.

Activity 6

Complete the spider diagram of the theme 'Love' that has been started below.

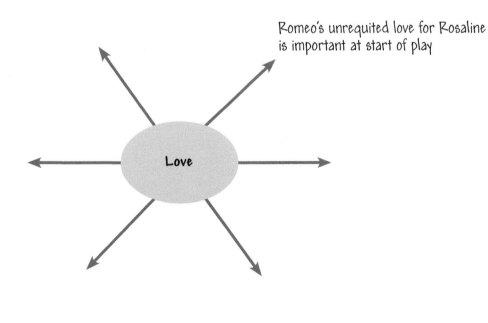

Romeo's unrequited love for Rosaline is important at start of play

Love

Answering questions in the exam

Appropriate language

Essays do not have to be written in a style that is extremely formal and academic in order to gain the highest marks. A clear and consistent style is needed in order that you effectively communicate to the examiner what you think about aspects of the play. Don't worry about crossings-out – the examiner will only assess the parts you indicate as your final answer.

juxtapose put next to something opposing for contrasting effect

You should avoid writing that Shakespeare 'says' or 'speaks about' something or someone in an essay. The use of these verbs in this context is too informal.

Activity 7

Look at the following list of verbs that can be used appropriately to describe what a writer 'does' in a text. You could also use these verbs to describe the effect of characters, a word, phrase, line, Act or Scene.

describes	argues (that)	thinks (that)	portrays
emphasises	dramatises	allows (us)	pictures
conveys (an idea)	knows (that)	depicts	creates
makes (us)	illustrates	reflects	stages
demonstrates (that)	recounts	shocks	understands
pleases (us)	focuses (upon)	states	juxtaposes
pities	examines	analyses	encourages (us to)
implies (that)	shows	senses (that)	warns (us that)
asks/answers	succeeds (by/in…)		

Notice that all the verbs are:

- in the present tense (because discussing the text is always in the moment)
- the 'us' refers to the audience in the context of the play, never the reader.

a) Which verbs would you use to describe the use of imagery?

- -

b) Which verbs relate to arguing a point?

----

c) Which verbs relate to emotion?

See how many other verbs of your own you can add to each list.

When using **conjunctions** in your essays to develop points, be careful of sounding too formulaic as this gives the impression of being too pre-planned. You should use conjunctions in a flexible way so that their use is natural for your style and appropriate for the tone of the essay. Avoid using 'firstly,… secondly,… thirdly …' if possible.

> **conjunction** a word used to connect clauses or sentences

The list below contains more formal conjunctions that can be used appropriately in your essays. Where there is an informal version of the word, this is placed in brackets to remind you of the alternative.

however (but)	furthermore (also)	additionally (also)
therefore (so)	although	initially (firstly)
whereas	similarly	for example (e.g.)
for instance (e.g.)	in conclusion	in other words/that is (i.e.)
alternatively	on the other hand	notwithstanding (even knowing that)
consequently	ultimately (finally)	nevertheless/nonetheless (anyway)

Most of these words or phrases can be used at the beginning of or within sentences. Practise using them and develop your style so that you are comfortable with them.

Activity 8

The following student response discusses Friar Lawrence in Act 2, Scene 3. Fill in the blank spaces with the most appropriate formal conjunctions.

> In Act 2, Scene 3 Friar Lawrence _____ believes that Romeo is still in love with Rosaline, _____ he soon realises that Romeo's 'dear love is set' on Juliet. _____, he struggles to understand the change in Romeo and that he has 'forsaken' his previous love. _____, he has to offer Romeo new advice and suggests that he take things 'Wisely and slow'.

Planning answers

You do not have time to plan an answer in detail in the exam. Your revision strategies, if effective, should have prepared you to be able to think quickly and to select appropriate ideas and quotations. However, a brief plan, taking one or two minutes, can help to organise your thinking. In this plan you should jot down ideas for an introduction, followed by main points and a conclusion.

Look at the brief plan below for an essay asking you to explore the presentation of Friar Lawrence in the play.

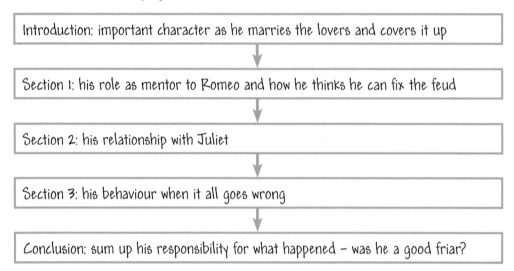

Introduction: important character as he marries the lovers and covers it up

Section 1: his role as mentor to Romeo and how he thinks he can fix the feud

Section 2: his relationship with Juliet

Section 3: his behaviour when it all goes wrong

Conclusion: sum up his responsibility for what happened – was he a good friar?

Note that:

- a plan like this cannot remind you of all the detail
- you can write more than one paragraph within a development section
- you do not have to follow it exactly – you can change your mind!

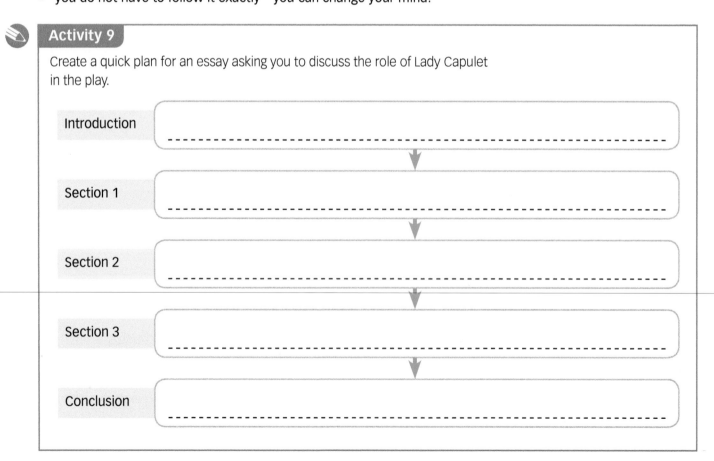

Activity 9

Create a quick plan for an essay asking you to discuss the role of Lady Capulet in the play.

Introduction

Section 1

Section 2

Section 3

Conclusion

Effective introductions

An introduction allows the examiner to see the range of points you intend to discuss. The subjects you raise and the knowledge you show, even if briefly, should demonstrate that you can handle the material confidently and have a strong overview and grasp of the text.

You should:

- show that you have clearly understood the question
- summarise the points you will be looking at in more detail later in the essay
- demonstrate an overview by referring to points throughout the text
- end by linking in to the subject of the next paragraph.

Look at the following sample exam question:

> Look again at Act 3, Scene 5.
>
> In this extract, Juliet says goodbye to Romeo just before her mother, Lady Capulet, comes to see her.
>
> **a)** Explore how Shakespeare presents Juliet's relationship with her mother in this extract. Refer closely to the extract in your answer.
>
> **b)** How is this relationship presented in the rest of the play?

The following are examples of introductions to essays attempting to answer this question:

Student A

Brief overview

Some analysis of her emotions with use of integrated quotation

In this scene Juliet is hiding something from her mother. She has just seen Romeo leave and is very upset because she has already seen him 'dead in the bottom of a tomb' and is worrying that she might not see him again. To make things worse, her mother has arrived and criticises her for still crying for Tybalt (i.e. what she thinks is the reason for the tears). Juliet pretends to her mother that she wants Romeo dead as revenge for Tybalt's death. She is pretending to agree with her mother because she cannot tell the truth. She has had a difficult relationship with her mother since she met Romeo. I will analyse this in more detail in the rest of this essay.

Shows understanding of plot twist

Focuses on the question

Things to improve:

- more comment needed on the relationship in the rest of the play
- more use of short quotations that reflect their relationship
- link more closely to the content of the next section.

Student B

Clear understanding and links to later events in the scene

Integrated quotation to reflect hierarchy in family

Integrated quotation to explore her underlying feelings

> This extract is the last time Juliet speaks to her mother before the devastating conflict with her father in the next scene. Juliet calls her 'my lady mother' in respect for her position but at this point does not really trust her because of the way she has referred to Romeo as 'villain' and 'the traitor murderer'. We know that Lady Capulet wanted Romeo killed after the fight with Tybalt and will still be angry that he has only been exiled to Mantua (promising to have him poisoned in a previous scene!). This extract marks a turning point in their relationship – the final time they talk before the marriage to Paris is reorganised. From the beginning of the play we are presented with quite a distant relationship between mother and daughter. We can only understand this scene in the context of what has gone before and this will be dealt with later in the essay. In the next section I wish to look more closely at how the language used in the scene by Lady Capulet reflects this distance and apparent lack of empathy.

Selected use of plot line to support analysis of character

Clear sense of overview

Reference to further analysis later in the essay

Direct link to the next section of the essay

Things to improve:

- some short quotations to reflect Lady Capulet's earlier cold and ruthless attitude in the play (asking the Prince for Romeo's 'blood' in revenge for Tybalt's death)
- more references to before and after the scene to develop the overview.

Activity 10

On a separate piece of paper, write an effective introduction to one of the following questions:

- Explore the presentation of the Nurse in *Romeo and Juliet*.
- Examine the ways that conflict is presented in *Romeo and Juliet*.
- What do you feel is the most important scene in the play? Explain your choice by comparing the effect of the scene with at least one other scene.

Effective conclusions

The conclusion should draw the essay to a logical close.

You should:

- show that you have clearly answered the question
- summarise the key points you have made through the essay (though try not to repeat the same sentence structures and vocabulary if possible)
- demonstrate a reflective sense of overview
- use some short quotations to clearly support points
- end the essay with a clear and well-supported analysis.

Activity 11

a) Read the following conclusion to a student's essay that is answering the sample exam question on page 91. Look at the comments suggesting how it could have been improved.

Student A

More analysis needed of why she is 'on her own'.

More explanation required and reference to Friar Lawrence.

Include a reference to an example of this.

> In this scene it is clearly obvious to the audience that Juliet is on her own in her family and that she can only rely on Romeo. In the rest of the play her mother has not been seen as very maternal and that is probably why Juliet is so naive and innocent in the way she does things. If she had been able to go and talk to her mother about her feelings instead of just the Nurse, things would have gone very differently in my opinion. She probably would not have ended up killing herself.

This idea is not supported and explained.

An unexplained assertion.

b) Now read the second student example below. Make notes on where and how you think it could be improved.

Student B

> Her father threatens to disown her, her mother gives her no support and the Nurse turns her back. Juliet and her mother are not acting like a mother and daughter in this scene. It is a turning point in their relationship and makes the audience understand why she feels so alone. In the rest of the play it is shown that Lady Capulet does not seem like a parent at all and it is no wonder that Juliet falls into the arms of Romeo – she has nowhere else to go.

----

c) Write your own conclusion to the same question. Try to avoid the weaknesses of the examples and leave the examiner feeling that you have a confident grasp of the text and can offer valid and well-supported points.

Progress check

Use the chart below to review the skills you have developed in this chapter.
For each column, start at the bottom box and work your way up towards the
highest level in the top box. Tick the box to show you have achieved that level.

I can sustain a critical response to *Romeo and Juliet* and interpret the language, characterization and themes convincingly ☐	I can analyse the effects of Shakespeare's use of language, structure and form in *Romeo and Juliet*, using subject terms judiciously ☐	I can use well-integrated textual references from *Romeo and Juliet* to support my interpretation ☐	I use a wide range of vocabulary and can spell and punctuate consistently accurately ☐
I can develop a coherent response to *Romeo and Juliet* and explain the language, characterization and themes clearly ☐	I can explain how Shakespeare uses language, structure and form to create effects in *Romeo and Juliet*, using relevant subject terms ☐	I can use quotations and other textual references from *Romeo and Juliet* to support my explanation ☐	I use a range of vocabulary and can spell and punctuate, mostly accurately ☐
I can make some comments on the language, characterization and themes in *Romeo and Juliet* ☐	I can identify some of Shakespeare's methods in *Romeo and Juliet* and use some subject terms ☐	I can make references to some details from *Romeo and Juliet* ☐	I use a simple range of vocabulary and spell and punctuate with some accuracy ☐
Personal response	**Language, structure, form**	**Textual references**	**Technical accuracy**

Glossary

ambiguity use of language that leaves the listener unsure of the actual meaning

antithesis a person or thing that is the direct opposite of another; in text, where words or phrases are deliberately placed in opposition to each other to reflect a particular mood

blank verse unrhymed lines of poetry with regular metre

Chorus in Elizabethan drama, an actor who recites the Prologue and may comment at other times on the action of the play

confidant (m)/confidante (f) someone who acts as a counsellor, someone to be trusted

conjunction a word used to connect clauses or sentences

dichotomy a division or contrast between two things that are different or in opposition

double entendre a word or phrase that is open to more than one interpretation; often used for sexual references

dramatic irony when the words or action of a scene are understood by the audience, but not by one or more of the characters on stage

dynastic marriage a marriage that strengthens family links

empathy the ability to understand and share the feelings of another

epitaph a short text honouring someone who has died, sometimes expressing a message, moral or warning

eponymous referring to the fact that the character's name forms part of the title of the play

extended metaphor a comparison between two things that runs on over several sentences or lines of a play or poem

hierarchy a system in which there is a clear ranking of groups or individuals, some having more power and status than others

homograph a word that has the same spelling and pronunciation but different meanings, e.g. *bow* (noun: a weapon used to fire arrows/the front section of a ship) and *bow* (verb: to show respect to royalty by bending forward from the waist)

homophone a word that sounds like another with a different meaning, e.g. *stake/steak*

iambic pentameter a line of verse with ten syllables, forming five 'feet', where the stress falls on the second syllable in each foot

juxtapose put next to something opposing for contrasting effect

melodramatic exaggerated or overemotional (i.e. lacking credibility)

metaphor a figure of speech applied to something to suggest a resemblance, without using the words 'like' or 'as'

patriarchy/patriarchal a system or society based on the dominance of men over women

personification when human qualities are given to something non-human, such as an object or idea

perspective a particular opinion or point of view that is dependent on personal interests or beliefs

Prologue in drama, an introductory scene, often written in verse, that establishes the themes, plot or characters of the play; from the Greek *pro* (before) and *logos* (word)

protagonist(s) the main character(s)

pun a type of joke or word play that relies on the similar sound but different meaning of words

rhyming couplets two consecutive lines that rhyme

simile a figure of speech applied to something to suggest a resemblance introduced by the words 'like' or 'as'

soliloquy where a character voices aloud their innermost thoughts for the audience to hear

sonnet a 14-line poem with a formal rhyme scheme and condensed form

tragedy a drama dealing with serious themes, ending in the suffering or death of one or more of the principal characters

Great Clarendon Street, Oxford, OX2 6DP, United Kingdom

Oxford University Press is a department of the University of Oxford.
It furthers the University's objective of excellence in research, scholarship,
and education by publishing worldwide. Oxford is a registered trade mark
of Oxford University Press in the UK and in certain other countries

British Library Cataloguing in Publication Data

Data available

ISBN 978-019-839887-5

10 9 8 7 6 5 4 3 2

Printed in Great Britain by CPI Group (UK) Ltd., Croydon CR0 4YY

Acknowledgements

The publisher and authors would like to thank the following
for permission to use photographs and other copyright material:

Cover: © Konstanttin/Shutterstock

Extracts are taken from the Oxford School Shakespeare: *Romeo and Juliet*,
edited by Roma Gill (OUP, 2008)